TEN
TRUTHS

A Profound Realization
of Life

STEVEN CONSIDINE

There is a door that opens when you are willing. THE OPEN DOOR PRESS May you find the courage to walk through it.

Book cover designed by Steven Considine

Interior layout by Steven Considine

Editing by Collen McSpirit-Bush

Paperback ISBN: 978-0-578-39092-5

Printed in the United States of America
First Printing, 2022
Second Printing, 2023

www.stevenconsidine.com
email: hellofriend@stevenconsidine.com

The Beginning

The Middle

The End

This book honors you
and anyone who seeks
a greater understanding
of themselves and their world.

This book is for
all those who have brought joy
and love into my life in endless ways;
my glorious family,
Tammy, Mackensi and Zoe.

This book, in deep gratitude,
recognizes the many teachers
who have guided me along the way,
and walk with me still.

It is not my voice that speaks alone,
but it is our Voice together,
that speaks
as One.

Here you will see
the face of Wisdom

You will feel
the joy of Love

You will know
the peace of Truth

Hello, Friend

I present this work to you - culminating a lifetime of walking the road to self-understanding and seeking peace in the world. I share with you all the trials and tribulations of being human: the daily necessity of making money to survive, having bills to pay and too often, more needs than resources. Like you, I share the same sweet will to be happy, to live in joy, feel safe, to love and be loved.

I know what it is to have a poor credit rating and go bankrupt; what it is to be depressed and lust after something you cannot have, to be enraged and wanna smash someone in the face. I have been desperate and alone, lost and confused, felt imprisoned and helpless and mourned death. Like most, there is much called negative life, I have encountered in some way.

And yet, I also know what it is to have money and pay your bills on time, to get along with your neighbors, obey the law and get A's in school. I have been a Boy Scout, altar boy, have pride in my country, gone to Church and prayed, raised and supported a family. I have seen the world and tasted the finer things, been at peace and in love. There is much of the good life I have also experienced. So, I am well-rounded in my living.

I am well-read, well-traveled, well-schooled, have done very well and am well-regarded. But also, have very well been contemptible and foolish.

All these things, both good and bad, are my thoughts and feelings, issues and problems, my failures and triumphs. They are the clouds that pass through the sky of my Being, that come and go, change shape and form. Sometimes they reflect intense beauty and other times madness. In moments, seemingly inspired by God and in others, a devil.

But they are not my Truth. They are appearances and reflections that arise from something deeper. There is a greater reality beyond them all, which is my real Self and yours.

I come to you as a friend uncovered, without the arrogance of righteousness or the mask of false knowing and yet, deeply secure in my experience. I am here to speak honestly of my understanding, that I might be helpful to those who read these words, who are walking the same road I walk and seeking the same answers I seek, for we are all on this journey together.

Here within is the Truth as I have come to know it. Is it the ultimate Truth? Most definitely not. But it is still valid, for in each part there is the whole. Within one completely true idea is the entirety of Existence.

The goal of this book is simple - to show the way to living a more fulfilling, self-empowered life, such as I have sought and found. This we achieve, through sorting out the false from the true and dispelling our illusions about Life and who we are in It.

We each now stand, fully alive in the present moment, all on the cusp of great potential. Why then not make the most of it? And what does that mean, but to experience Life completely, in the purity of itself, without fear or guilt, judgment, lack or limitation.

Many are content to live not questioning. There is no impulse to find any deeper meaning. The routines of daily life provide enough comfort and security, they don't consider if there is something more. And this is perfectly fine for them, for there is no right and wrong way to live, only being as happy as we can with what we have.

For me, however; I am most satisfied when I come to some deeper realization about myself or the world.

I could tell you, one day I was sitting in meditation, opened my eyes to see a Being of Light standing there, who imparted to me the secrets of the universe. How spiritual that would sound and how holy I would be. But that hasn't happened and probably never will. I really have no story to tell. I am not special. I am an ordinary person. Life causes us all to seek answers. Though, most are not willing to wait and listen. I did and it is only that, which has made the difference.

I am one who has traveled the long road to sanity. For some, this is not glamorous, or movie material and no burning bush. But it is honest and so, something you can trust with all your heart.

What I speak about here is real and within my words lies the doorway for anyone to come to a greater realization. If I can climb the mountain to understanding what is stopping you, but for the effort? Only willingness is required. How valuable is knowing, for Knowledge is Power and don't we all seek the power to live a fulfilled Life?

This is what I have known - I did not have the kindest of upbringings. My father was an abusive alcoholic my whole childhood and my mother was never fully present. He finally became sober when I was in my teens - she left and they divorced. But by then, the damage was done.

I will say, like too many others, I grew up feeling unloved and unsafe and eventually, such despair became intolerable. At the time, I could medicate that pain, run from those nightmares, hide from myself or face my demons, and at some point, I did them all.

Though, from that grief and terror grew an intense desire to find the answers to living a happier life; out of that great inner struggle grew wisdom.

I discovered what worked and didn't work. I have learned, if one chooses, they can be healed of all pain and suffering from the past, not partly, but completely. For a long time, this seemed impossible to me. Today, not only is it possible, it is my life. You may well ask, am I now totally at peace? Wholly joyful? Utterly fulfilled? The answer is Yes!

But does that mean I don't have moments of unrest and disquiet? I longer experience fear and guilt, anger and sorrow? The answer is No!

When I am at peace, I am in the deep stillness of peace. When I am joyful, I am overflowing with Joy. When I am upset, I am upset. But now, it is tempered by the realization of a deeper knowing. When I am unhappy, my unhappiness is now eased by the remembrance of a greater joy. When I am afraid, my fear is felt more lightly, in understanding all experiences are chosen. I am in a place I've been to many times before. Here is where I have had the most difficulty and yet, it is also here I have found the greatest clarity.

I no longer tremble in the dark, but embrace it, for it is the darkness that causes us to seek the Light and it is in the Light that our True Self is found.

I am not a work in progress, neither are you. We are all complete, perfect and whole. What is incomplete is the manifestation of that perfection in the world. This is true for everyone. No matter what we encounter or experience, it changes not the purity of our Inner Beingness. My past does not define me, no more than does yours define you. Herein lies total healing.

Does it not interest you to find freedom from all limitations and live happily in the world? Don't you yearn for peace and dream of the day when you are free of fear and guilt?

Doesn't your heart burn with the desire to Live in the Light of Love always, to feel no lack, no worry, no trepidation for the future? All this and more does Truth bring to those who realize it and in accepting it, live their lives by it. For such a glorious gift as this, is given to those who dare open the door to self-understanding. It is yours, but for the asking.

How long does it take? How long does it take for the light of the Sun to fill a darkened room? But an instant! It is only getting up from the chair, walking across the floor, unlocking the bolt, turning the knob and opening the door that seems to take all the time in the world.

I would urge you then, put to test what I have written. Take not what I say at face value, but see it work in your own life, in your own way and find what is waiting your invitation to enter. For it is only through our own experience, can we finally know the truth of our Self.

I am here as your friend, and you as mine, and together we have created this world as it seems to be. Should we not pause a moment, every day, and ask ourselves what can we do to make it a brighter place for ourselves, our children and their children to come?

The path begins not by trying to change the world, but first transforming our own hearts and minds. Then, when we are set aright, we can work to right the wrongs ignorance makes.

Know this: There is no darkness so impenetrable, the Light cannot dispel it; no suffering so deep, Love cannot not heal the pain; no problem so vast, a Solution cannot be found; no question so perplexing, an Answer cannot be given and no despair so great, that Hope cannot rise up and bring us Peace.

I know it is hard to waken from the long, slumbering dream of hopelessness that can entrap us and keeps us bound to fear and misery. It is not an easy road we travel. But it is a necessary one. There are no magic answers in life, but there are those that are Miraculous.

It is my promise, by the end of this work, you will never see life the same again and you will be grateful for that new vision.

Seek then and find, ask and receive, for all the Universe is blessed in your listening.

Steven

So it began

I usually sleep in when on vacation. That morning though, I rose before sunrise and was wide awake. I tossed back and forth, trying to keep dreaming but to no avail. My thoughts kept turning to the world outside. I have learned to listen when that inner voice calls and so I got up and dressed, opened the creaking door as quietly as I could and ventured out into the dawn. I crept over the yard of lush green grass and down a winding stone path. I ended up in a clearing at the water's edge and found a comfortable spot to sit.

Across the lake, the mountains rose up before me covered with pine trees, standing tall like spires of a living cathedral. A mist floated over the peaks descending down the long slopes to flow gently across the calm surface of the water. The air was crisp and clean and there was a deep stillness present. I drifted off into thought.

I began to think about this beautiful landscape and how it had been here for millions of years. Yes, the trees were not that old, neither the water that filled the basin. But, the mountains were. The dirt under my feet and the sky over my head was.

Imagine I wondered, the many generations before me who had seen this valley. How long have humans walked on these very banks, from before the stone age to the modern world? So many cultures have risen up on its plateaus and fallen down, only the ruins can count.

Who else had sat on this rock? A soldier off to war in Europe, taking one last glance at home. A slave having escaped the prison of the south and seeing freedom and hope everywhere. A colonist spying out the movements of the British to warn the rebels of their advance. An Indian of a native tribe out seeking the morning's game. And so many more we know nothing about. And each with their own view.

I tried to feel the vastness of years this planet has existed and the untold trillions of lives lived here. I trembled before the magnitude of it all. My mind was grasping for comprehension, reaching out to understand this immeasurable existence.

But I saw how futile that was. I came to an impasse in my thinking and was painfully frustrated. How could I possibly grasp the universe this way? Or hold all the ocean in a cup? It cannot be logically grasped. Still I needed an answer.

Within me, I felt a gentle pull towards surrender, to letting go and so, having developed a deep trust in that inner knowing I released my mind, instead focusing all my attention on the scene playing out before me.

Smooth like glass was the surface of water, with delicate little wisps of vapor floating aimlessly by. Looking closer I could see a swarm of tiny insects hovering close to the shore line. They seemed so intent on their activity. Underneath, small fish darted frantically here and there. I marveled at the amazing life that was everywhere.

Suddenly, the hushed silence was broken by a loud cry. Far off in the distance an egret took flight from the branch of a fallen tree. Its white wings spread out and extended, to embrace the currents of cool morning air. Like a dancer, it moved effortlessly across the lake, with each thrust of its wings climbing higher and higher as though filled with an unseen power. I watched entranced by its graceful movements and felt an intimate connection between us, almost as though I too were flying with it, soaring joyfully through the sky.

I was overtaken by the most exquisite sense of beauty and rightness. Quietly above, the first rays of the sun broke across the rugged faces of stone and washed over the still surface below. It was then I realized how ancient the world is and long have been the days of the Earth. Yet, with every sunrise there is Life - abundant Life - new and untarnished in the fullness and glory of Itself, undiminished by time or process.

We can never appreciate human existence as it was or will be. It can only be understood now, because we are Now and it is we who give it meaning. All that has gone before is gone. What is Here is all that is here. Time is a carpet and when walking down, the past rolls up, as the future unfolds. But, our feet are always standing in the present and this we can comprehend.

I felt it then, that sense of eternalness I was trying to grasp, but can only be known in the moment we are living. By being fully present, I could feel the Presence of Everlasting Life surrounding me and with it a deep abiding sense of peace. I had my answer, not in words or ideas but in direct experience.

I sat for a while longer, fully immersed in the tranquility of that morning. I thought about the great distance I traveled to be able to sit here and know the purpose of my life. I thought of all the years of struggle, of practice, seeking, yearning and how I found Truth within that Presence. Finally, I was at a place where I felt some deeper level of understanding perhaps worth sharing.

I believe a great teacher is first a great student. We cannot rush through life, pretending to have knowledge we did not gain ourselves, just to seek for honor, where honor is not earned. It is only after we have walked the road, that nearing its end, are we capable of guiding others in the right direction.

For me, I sensed it was time to write down what I have learned, because Clarity belongs to everyone who seeks for happiness and peace and a more profound realization of Life.

I took out the notebook I always carry, opened it to the middle and wrote at the top of the page, "Some Fundamental Truth." I didn't know what would come next. I felt Understanding within me and let it guide me in my writing. I wrote for a good hour and stopped when I sensed someone looking over my shoulder.

"Dad, what are you doing?" My oldest daughter, Mackensi asked, her arms stationed on her hips somewhat scoldingly, my youngest daughter standing right behind her. "We have been looking all over for you. "

"Yeah Dad," Zoe chimed in. "We've been looking all over for you."

"I didn't want to wake anyone up., I replied glancing backwards.

"Well we are hungry and want to get breakfast. "

"That's a great idea," I said closing my notebook, then getting up and giving them both a big hug and kiss. "I am starving."

Mackensi grinned and all her fake annoyance melted away.

"So why did you get up so early?" she asked, as we all walked together up the winding stone path back to the lodge.

I wondered what to say that would make sense, but I was without words. "That's a great question," I answered.

"Finally," Tammy said, greeting us at the top of the hill. "What have you been up to?" she asked inquisitively.

I laughed. How could I explain it to them? "Just one of those things." I smiled. "One of those things we have to do now and then."

Someday, they would know the real answer.

SECTION ONE

Some Fundamental Truth

This book is all about the Truth. But what is truth? Truth is the way Life is. So, it would seem simple enough, to know how things are all we have to do is look out our window. Why do we need to be told what should be obvious? And quite honestly, I have puzzled over this question for many decades.

For me, I could never understand how our species has lived for this long and there is still much about ourselves we don't know. We often hear reports of the latest breakthroughs. But humans have not changed for eons. Are they really discovering anything new or what already exists?

Why are we not born with the knowledge of how we function? It seems a mystery, the body is more advanced than the conscious mind. Who orders the healing of a wound? What directs the heart to pump blood? There is a vast field of physical functioning we are completely unaware of and yet, still operates.

How possible though, is this? Unless there are aspects to our self, we don't comprehend. Maybe then, what we are is not so apparent. If we want to know the Truth of human existence, we must look again, perhaps a little deeper.

There is another level of being, beyond our normal awareness. But to reach that depth, we have to begin where we are and start with the fundamentals.

Most think they have a real understanding of life and in some respects we do. We know how to eat and drink, to walk and talk. All the physical mechanisms we grasp so well and yet, there are larger truths which passeth our understanding.

We are so focused on outer activities, that we fail to pay attention to our inner existence and it is really there, where Being lives. If more of us gave time to discovering the world within, the world without would be a vastly different place.

Too often, because we lack awareness, we are the victim of our experience and not its conscious creator. But this need not be. Who wants to be a victim of anything? No one. We all want to be the master of our fate. And why shouldn't we? We each have the power of decision over our lives.

What I have come to understand is this - while reality is not hidden, knowledge of its true nature can be forgotten and has to be remembered. This seems to be the very essence of our world.

In autumn the leaves fall and flowers bury underground, waiting to sprout in the spring. Clouds come and go, only to come again. It is the cycle of life here. Understanding is released and found anew in a different time, a different culture, speaking in different symbols.

If we do not breathe out, we cannot breathe in. The truth of living always passes and is reborn as the living truth of a new generation.

So, here we are rediscovering what has always existed and is like a new blossom on an ancient tree; still soft and fragrant, still delicate and yet everlasting. Let us begin then, regaining those lost memories of Truth.

Fundamental Truth One

What am I?

What are we? Such a basic question. What do we know about someone when meeting them? We size them up and see what they look like. Are they tall or short, fat or skinny? What color hair do they have? Do they even have hair? Are they wearing glasses? How old are they? Are they male or female?

Though we are only describing the attributes of a human being. But, are body characteristics alone, what defines us? If we approached someone on the street and asked, "Who are you?" what would their response be?

Some might answer the question with their name, others with their position in society or their profession. Who are you? I am Steven. I am someone's son. What are you? I am a teacher. I am this religion, or that orientation. The list of descriptions is endless and depending on the mood, or circumstance, who we say we are is never the same.

It is obvious what the physical self is – an organism that consumes nutrients, turning those elements into energy. It's a vehicle that needs fuel to move around, whose goal is to continue moving around and because its actions are purposeful, we say it's alive.

When we refer to the body, we often describe its condition. Is it toned, or out of shape, does it ache or feel good? Sometimes, we describe its characteristics. It can be who we are, or what we have. Though, there is always a sense of more, another level of identity.

I am a human being, defines me as being tangible. I am a good person, identifies me as something conceptual.

What I am is a physical being.
Who I am is a person.

A person is not a thing but a concept. In simple terms, who we are, is what we define ourselves to be.

Many believe the brain is the source of self. But where in the vast number of cells is identity kept? What part gives rise to that feeling of me?

The truth is, that which states I AM is not an aspect of physicality, nor does it arise from all the activities of material life. Selfhood is in the realm of abstract thinking and where does thinking occur but in the mind.

In the world, we are flesh and blood, bone and muscle. Though, our deeper nature transcends corporeal existence. All of us recognize who we are in the mirror. But that can be despairing, when we believe our entire identity lies only in what we see.

The body has no grand motivation. It does not seek for inner peace, yearn for enlightenment, or love, nor to understand the origins of the universe. In our humanness, our one goal is existing.

What we are determines our purpose. What our function is, decides our meaning. If we are just what a reflection shows, then we are limited and what we seek after, crave for, or care about, will be focused solely on survival.

But how meaningful is this? The body does not advance to any higher state of being. Every day is the same routine of eating, drinking, breathing and sleeping. There is no long-term gain. What we did before, has no bearing on what we do now. The food we ate yesterday, does not fill us today. It is an ongoing cycle that does not end. We cannot retire from meeting the body's needs and up to our last moment we will be hungry, only in death are we done.

How frail is such a life, that losing our breath for a few minutes can end it all? Does that make us feel safe and at peace? We can begin to see, identifying our entire existence with the physical process, lends itself to feelings of despair, trepidation and hopelessness. Is this really Living?

Thankfully though, we are more than what appearance shows. If there is one transforming Idea to begin changing our life and in

realizing the Truth, it is that we are not just a body, but also a mind.
Who am I?

Who we are is not so much a thing, as a non-thing. If it was said,
we are an Idea, it would seem to imply we are less real than a car, a
boat or a chair. That is because we cannot see or grasp the mind or
its effects and are taught to believe, only what we can touch and feel
is real.

Yet, being a good person or a writer, or someone of means are all
mental images. True, they may describe something in the world, but
they are really non-physical ideas. It is not the brain that thinks and
where those concepts are held. Mind is the creator of thought and
the bastion of identity.

What is mind?

Mind cannot be described as an object, neither seen or measured, weighed or delineated. It has no material properties. It is not
subject to the laws of time and space. It is best understood as similar
elements are - radio waves, radiation and light - as forms of energy.

The mind is a structure of energy, where experience is felt. More
so, it is aware of itself as a living entity and being conscious, it holds
the truth of its nature as its identity. That sense of self we so often
attribute to the body, is really an aspect of the Energy we are.

What am I?

I am a body, but also a mind.

I am matter but also energy.

I am, at once, both a physical and non-physical being.

Fundamental Truth Two

I am a Being of Energy

What is Energy?

Energy is almost indefinable. It is the creator and the created. The mover and the moved. It is the defined but surpasses definition. Energy is Cause and everything its effect.

We are beings of Energy. We are that which precedes and sustains all forms. In truth, there is no separation between physical and non-physical existence, between body and mind. Energy is the primary substance of all things. As it expands, it manifests itself in multiplicity of ways.

We are more than just forces that move. We have mindful intention. There are many names to describe what cannot be put into words – the soul, spirit, beingness, eternal consciousness. But whatever the term, it is only a means to understand what is beyond human comprehension. Though, still within the grasp of our experience.

Foremost, we are conscious beings and what is consciousness, but awareness of reality. What is reality? It is the field of energy where life is experienced, encompassing everything that exists.

As human beings, our awareness tends to be limited to the world. Often, we are blind to what lies beyond our physical self, because we only believe in what we can see. So, we assume there is nothing else to know. But obviously, there is more.

What is the Self?

As our energy is manifested in form, so does our Consciousness have both physical and non-physical identity. The self we know is the person that lives the human life. But there is a greater Beingness from which we emerge.

If this is true and it is, how can we be something we have no knowledge of? If we are this being of Energy that exists beyond normal experience, why don't we know it?

When you are in a valley, your view is limited. But, as you climb a mountain you begin to discover more, until finally, you reach the peak and see the whole landscape below. Human existence is a plateau of consciousness. Our experience of reality is therefore constrained, to a certain level of awareness.

We are one self, not divided into separate parts. Our minds, however, can focus on a single point, to the exclusion of everything else. Our life in the world is really a specific focus of the expanded Mind that we are. So, we are not fully aware of our total reality for this reason. We can, if we choose, realize more of this Wholeness and have a greater appreciation of the life we are living.

This is the road all humanity walks – the return to the awareness of the greater Self. Most do it without recognizing the path they are on. Some, see a flash of light on the mountaintop and are curious to see what it is. Either way, our very nature compels us to seek growth.

Everything in life is a journey; a step by step process where one realization leads to the next and new understanding is built on the knowledge already gained. But we always begin at the beginning and climb the ladder of recognition one rung at a time.

True expansion of consciousness comes not from seeing God in Heaven. It is looking within our self, discovering who we are in day to day life, under ordinary circumstances and coming to a deeper insight into human existence.

It is not heralded like the coming of a king or queen. It arrives unannounced; a surprise visitor dropping by and bringing with them the most magnificent news, that will change your life forever.

Fundamental Truth Three

Function determines our body's condition.
Feelings determine our state of mind.

In essence, our reality is the circumstances we live. As a two-part being, we have physical and nonphysical aspects that affect our daily life. We call these overall conditions, the state we are in.

What determines the state of the body?

Is our body hot or cold, wet or dry? Are we at rest, moving, sitting or standing still? Such factors decide outer physical experience.

Does our heart beat in regular rhythm, blood flows, air inhaled and exhaled out? Is the stomach breaking down food? Are the liver and kidneys filtering impurities? These processes determine our internal condition.

If the inner mechanisms are working correctly, we say the body is healthy. If not, it is sick. When our environment fulfills our needs, life is good. Otherwise, it is called bad.

Our physical state is judged on the effectiveness of taking in raw materials and converting them to energy. We eat, drink and breathe, so we can move around. Its functioing then, is determined by its ability to fulfill that purpose.

But what determines the state of our mind?

If the mind were just an effect of the brain and we were only physical beings, when the body was good, we would be happy. But this is not always true.

It is quite common to be healthy and yet our mind can be in distress. Or, we can be at peace, even when the body is sick or dying. So, if the physical body is not the Self, then its condition does not create our inner state.

The mind is never hot or cold, thirsty or hungry, in motion or at rest. It can be happy or sad, at peace, in conflict, confused or desperate, fearful or loving. All these circumstances we say, is how we are feeling. Emotions then, are the indication of the mind's condition.

What creates our feelings,
determines the mind's state.

What are feelings and where do they come from?

Physical feelings are sensations of the outside world, experienced through sight, touch, smell and taste. Or, from within ourselves as pain or pleasure.

Emotional feelings, however, are non-physical and do not arise from the senses. A certain smell or texture does not make us feel a certain way. The scent of roses can't make us happy, or the odor of decay bring despair. A rough blanket doesn't cause discomfort, or a silk sheet bring arousal, unless we think they should. All emotions, regardless of their physical counterpart, come from what we think about our experience.

It is assumed by many, the brain thinks, because when we have a thought, the body instantly reacts. They are so seamlessly interconnected, we don't see them as separate, but the same. Though, they are different. The brain can and does process physical information. But it cannot deliberate, ponder, imagine or dream.

Thinking is the mind's activity. It is the creation of energy patterns we call thoughts, whose experience within the mind we call feelings.

Thoughts are patterns of energy.
The experience of energy
within the mind, we call feelings.
Feelings are an indication of our state of mind.

Energy in its primary nature is movement. Thoughts, as vibrations of consciousness, are not seen, but felt. They begin within the mind and ripple outward, like stones dropped in a calm pool, creating waves as they go. Some are harmonic, some discordant. But all leave an impression.

Feelings are sounds the mind makes when thinking. You hear them with your Being, not your ears.

Fundamental Truth Four

What we think we feel

This is perhaps, the most crucial understanding about our state of mind. If we are happy, it is because our thinking makes us happy. If we are sad or upset, it is our thoughts that made us sad or upset. Here is a powerful Truth – What we feel and experience within, is a consequence of what we believe and not a result of our physical condition or environment.

What creates our mental state?

It has been demonstrated in many ways, the brain can and does effect consciousness, or the awareness of the body. Anesthesia is a prime example of this. Drinking and taking drugs is another. But what has never been proven is, the body can alter the mind.

We cannot take a pill and suddenly believe something we didn't before. We cannot ingest certain fluids and be a different person. There is no magic potion that changes who we are. We can take medicine for depression or anxiety and because they have a chemical effect, believe we are cured. But the body is just a vehicle for the nonphysical self.

If a self-destructive person gets behind the wheel of a car, they may drive themselves off a cliff. We can certainly prevent that, by removing the gas from the tank or hiding the keys. But, that in no way changes their self-destructiveness. In the same manner, altering the body's chemistry does not heal the mind.

Our physical being is just a shadow cast over the canvas of the world. If we change our shape - our state of mind, we change our shadow - the body. We cannot alter Cause though, by manipulating its effects.

Our state of mind is determined by our thoughts and not our circumstances.

We are taught early on to believe, the opposite is true, that circumstances decide how we feel. It seems logical to say, if I am covered in mud, I must feel dirty; having no money makes me feel poor; in the middle of crisis, I must feel desperate. This list is endless.

It would also appear insane to say, even though my house burned down I am happy; in the middle of a war zone I am at peace; though others are persecuting me I am still filled with forgiveness.

Truth is the truth whether it appears logical or not. External conditions, no matter what they are, cannot make us feel a certain way. It is only what we believe about them, that determines our emotional state.

Here is one of Life's greatest blessing in freeing us from every misery, pain or suffering we will ever know. If circumstances are not the source of our feelings, then we are not at the mercy of forces beyond our control. Though we may not recognize it, still we always have a choice and having choices is power and freedom.

Fundamental Truth Five

What we think is a reflection of what we believe

Why do we think what we think?

It seems a mystery why people think one way and others another, why some are more positive and those more negative. Is this by chance or luck? Is it our DNA or how we were raised?

All thinking, from the smallest idea on the most trivial subject, to the grandest matter, follows the same law of mind.

Thoughts are not random or chaotic. They do not arise from the hidden recesses of our subconscious, to intrude upon the waking mind, only to disappear back into the unknown.

If we examine our inner contents, we discover, though we have many thousand thoughts a day and most appear quite unrelated, they all follow general patterns.

Thinking is creating and the mind does not create arbitrarily. Each thought originates from a sponsoring idea, which is a strongly held conviction we assume is true. In one way or another, all thoughts arise from something we believe.

It seems, what we think, is a reaction to our experience in the world. If I'm having happy thoughts, it is because I have something wanted; negative thoughts, I lost something valued. Dark thoughts come when life is difficult - I have no job, no relationship, no hopes for the future. Positive thinking means good things are happening for me. But truthfully, we feel a certain way, because we believe we should.

All circumstances elicit a reaction. We cannot avoid ruminating over the situations we are in and it is those perceptions that form our emotional response.

Events and circumstances cause us to think.

What we think reflects what we believe.

What we believe determines how we feel.

Why do we believe what we believe?

There are many reasons, but from the beginning, our parents teach us their belief system. In a sense, it acts like a family tradition handed down from generation to generation. It ensures social continuity, but later in life can become very limiting.

As children, we do not contradict adults and what they teach we regard more as knowledge and fact, than opinion. Rarely do we consider, a belief is just an idea. For us, they are truth and never doubted. And because they are accepted without question, they become the hidden foundation of our life.

Influences abound in youth - at school, on the playground, in the media and the world around us. Ultimately though, it is our own experience that defines what we hold as truth.

Yet, what thought system we accumulate over time, is not as important as how and why we maintain it. Beliefs, by their very nature, are subjective. They are concepts about Life and may not necessarily reflect reality. Therefore, they have to be reiterated and reinforced to continue being believed. Truth needs no defense, but perceptions certainly do.

If the sun were shining, we don't say, I think the sun is shining. That's a fact beyond debate. But if we said, "It's gorgeous out." That's an opinion.

The shining sun is not literally beautiful. Some might consider it the worst thing ever. Perhaps, a farmer during a drought would see it as a curse. A cloudy day might be a blessing instead, bringing much needed rain. It all depends on our perspective.

What is true, is always true regardless of our point of view. Perception, however, is based on our beliefs about reality and not on knowing.

Some people are convinced the Earth is flat, aliens visit the planet on a daily basis and bigfoot roams the forests. Everyone harbors ideas about life that are untrue. Yet, they will center their decisions around them and live according to their dictates.

We can believe what is true is true.

We can believe what is true is false.

We can believe what is false is false.

We can believe what is false is true.

All belief is a choice.

Fundamental Truth Six

It is our perception,
that determines our experience of the world

We are not forced into belief. Everything the mind thinks, at some point, was accepted. Most often, we have faith in what we are taught, because we trust those teaching us; we see them as life's authority, who are more knowledgeable, wiser, and know better. So naturally, we assume what they say, is the way it is.

No one believes to be true, what they think is false. It is how the mind works – because we believe it, it must be true. Therefore, our thinking becomes our reality.

As energy, the mind holds every thought as real, whether it is valid or not and we feel the full effect of those ideas. We assume then, because we experience them emotionally and see their effects, they must be right.

Beliefs are validated by feelings.

To really grasp belief as choice, it's important to understand how we encounter the world. There is the physical interaction through our senses and the mental-emotional experience within our mind.

How do we know when it is raining? We see it with our eyes or feel it on our skin. If the wind is blowing? It is the same. But when asked, what do we believe about it raining, or the blowing wind, there is always a decision that has to be made.

A sunny day can mean something good for a beach goer or bad for someone else. A windy day can be great for sailing and terrible for picnics. It's all relative, depending on our perception.

The difference between knowing and perceiving is simply this - in knowing there is no choice, what is known is known. In perception, however, there is only choice; what is perceived must be interpreted or given meaning.

Sunshine is waves of energy being expelled from the sun and reaching the Earth as both heat and light. Yet, we don't know if that is good or bad, right or wrong, pleasant or not pleasant. We decide what it means and that decision creates our experience.

On a cloudless summer day, in the middle of a dry and parched field, a man stood in great despair, because it was another day it did not rain. His crops were not nourished and did not grow.

Without healthy corn, he could not sell them at market and make the money he needs to pay his mortgage. He was terrified the bank would repossess his farm and his family would have no place to live.

On the same cloudless day, on a beach somewhere in the Caribbean, a man knelt happily in front of a camera, because it was another day it did not rain. He could get the pictures he needed to complete his assignment and get paid. He was at ease, knowing he would be able to pay his bills that month.

A woman in California is unhappy it is pouring out, because she can't go running in the park and was hoping to bump into someone she has on crush. So, she is Devastated and is alone again.

There is a boy in Wisconsin who is annoyed the camping trip is still on and he can't go because he's sick. If it was raining, it would have been postponed and most likely he would be able to go another day.

Within each person's experience of the same facts, there is an underlying reason why they respond and feel the way they do. It is not the event itself, but what they believe the circumstance means, for them.

The world outside,
does not make
the world inside.

Fundamental Truth Seven

Perception defines meaning

There is no absolute meaning to the world. For absolute is something that is always the same, under all conditions. We know when the sun shines and how it shines, but not the meaning of a shining sun.

Of itself, the physical universe is just a process. We decide whether something is good or bad, beneficial to us or not, a happy or sad event. We give it all the significance it has, for nothing of form has a set truth. It is the vehicle of expression, not what is expressed.

We cannot endure a meaningless life though, for meaninglessness is a lack of emotional experience, the void of nonbeing. As a physical/nonphysical entity, to live fully, we have to both see and feel.

Perception is seeing. But it is how we interpret what we see, that gives circumstances and events, their content.

How do we interpret our perceptions?

There has to be some basis, for how we see the world. It is not haphazard. There is a reason behind all of our choices.

We know, what we think is governed by what we believe. Since perception is just another way of describing what we think, it is our beliefs then, which form our perceptions.

Each belief we hold is not self-contained and is interdependent on the rest. They are not random or chaotic but organized in a structure. A good analogy is a tree.

Thoughts are like leaves that sprout from the limb of a belief. Such limbs grow from a larger branch and branches emerge from the trunk itself. So, while some thoughts seem completely unrelated, actually they are all joined at a common source.

The core of our thinking – the trunk of our tree – is comprised of the most strongly held ideas we hold, from which all else arises.

These are the concepts of what and who we are. It is our self image that is the foundation of our entire thought system.

All the thoughts we have, every feeling we experience, every belief we cherish, is directly related to this central idea.

If perceptions are reflections of beliefs and beliefs together form a personal identity, we can say our vision of the world is a result of who we think we are.

As we perceive, so we feel.
What we feel, we first believe.
What we believe, is who we are.

Fundamental Truth Eight

What we see in the world, we first see in our self.

What we see outside ourselves, merely reflects what is within. If our entire thought system is founded on what and who we believe we are, it becomes obvious, how we perceive the world and all its events, is how we first see our self.

The material universe inspires no feeling because it has no personal meaning. The shining sun is just a nuclear reaction. The wind blowing is just the movement of air. Our physical living is only a process of taking in fuel, transforming it into energy, and using that to get more fuel.

What is the meaning in that? Nothing, it has none. But we live everyday with a purpose. Otherwise we could not continue, for a meaningless life has no value and what has no value is thrown away. Human existence is meaningful because we make it so.

How do we give meaning to the world and to ourselves?

The world we live in seems to exist apart from us. When someone is born, the world is the same. When someone dies, the world is the same. Our behavior can impact the planet but cannot change what it is. Through the entire span of our years, the world is the same.

Yet, in a very real sense we create it in each moment. Earth is the backdrop of our day-to-day existence. It is the canvas we use to paint the picture of our life; the blank page on which the story of who we are is written.

When we ask ourselves, "Who am I?" It is through daily circumstances, lifetime events and our relationships with others, that question is answered.

How we define conditions is a statement of who we are. Any event from the most mundane, to the life altering is relative to our individual perception.

Being given a million dollars, means something else to some-one who is poor, than someone who is rich. The poor person who has struggled to make ends meet and seen themselves as lacking and worthless, suddenly feels abundant and powerful. Their whole self-perception has changed and now envisioning their life, they are overjoyed.

A wealthy person, who is bequeathed the same amount of money, might consider it an insult compared to the family fortune and cer-tainly not, life changing. Perhaps now, they view themselves as less valued and this makes them angry and depressed.

Having a lot of money or little money is a physical circumstance that does not mean anything in itself. True, in the world, money has a great influence on what we can and cannot do. But, does being limited in action make us less valuable?

It is always about how we interpret conditions and not the con-ditions themselves that determines what they are.

Fundamental Truth Nine

We see the meaning of the world and our self
with our minds, not our eyes.

Perception, or how we see the world with our minds, is a process. When perceiving what is outside itself, the mind acts in an organized progression of steps, so quickly it goes unnoticed.

First, we acknowledge the circumstances we are in and recognize our situation.

Second, we decide what those circumstances mean to us and about us.

Third, we experience how that makes us feel.

Last, we decide to act on those feelings or not.

Whatever the circumstance, we decide what it means, by deciding who we are in that situation.

If we think we're a weak person, we interpret difficult events as overwhelming and we will despair, not knowing what to do, believing we cannot do it alone.

If we believe we are capable, able to meet whatever comes our way, we see difficulties as a challenge and are willing to do what needs be done. We feel determined not defeated.

Whenever we are afraid, it is not because circumstances are inherently fearful. But that we believe, we cannot overcome those conditions, because at some level we see our self as limited and powerless.

A bill comes in the mail. It is more money than I have in my account. Am I afraid because I can't make the payment, or am I determined to get what I need? How I see myself will decide how I feel and determine my actions. Our self-concept is the central factor we use to give meaning to the world around us.

Beliefs are just ideas about reality and not facts. But, what we believe, we hold as truth. Otherwise, we could not emotionally experience our thoughts. So how then do we decide what is true and what is not?

How is a belief system proven true?

In the physical world we prove something true or false from investigation and its results. Scientists test theories and look for evidence to validate their ideas. The mind operates the same way. It holds a belief and looks to the outer world for proof of its truth or falsity.

Here, however, is where the mind differs. It has a bias, towards its thought system. So, what we encounter, we interpret to be in alignment with our beliefs and what is not in agreement we dismiss.

The mind is not a neutral observer. It is a creator. We decide the world we want to see and create that world through our intepretations. In perception, we never see anyone or anything as they are, only as we want them to be.

Most think there is an independent world out there. We don't create it, it creates us. All our feelings, thoughts and beliefs are caused by what it is, not what we are. But the opposite is true.

Earth is a physical place of form and process. It is not good or bad, a happy or miserable planet to live on. Its purpose lies in the function we give it. So, if we say the world causes us to be who we are, then who we are is nothing. But that we live a life of sorrow and sadness, joy and wonder is evidence, we are more than just a body.

Belief creates perception.
Perception defines what we experience.
What we experience reinforces what we believe.

The world is not independent from us, though it appears to exist on its own. But, this is only true in physical form, where all things are inherently separate. But, as both Energy, we are One and everything is joined together.

In our minds, we hold the concept of who we are. We then take that idea and project it out, interpreting what we see and do as evidence our ideas are valid. Believing what we think we are seeing is true, we feel those emotions and it is those feelings that uphold our vision of ourself and the world.

Fundamental Truth Ten

We are the Creator of our experience

This is a world of cause and effect. Nothing happens here without a reason. Every situation we find ourselves in, every circumstance we encounter and event we experience, all result from a Cause.

What causes our life experiences?

For us, the reason behind everything is two-fold. Actions determine events and perceptions determine experience.

Some things that happen are the consequence of our behavior. We make a decision. It has an outcome. We may not always recognize our role in the process, but nevertheless, it is there.

If I live by a river and one day it overflows, flooding my house. It seems I had no role in the matter. Of course, we did not cause the flood. But we chose to live on its banks, knowing the potential of flooding. No one forced us there.

What is not so obvious is, a belief is also a decision. We encounter many things that seem out of our control. On the highway, we are in our lane, when someone drives in front of us and we have to swerve to avoid an accident. Certainly, we did not create that situation and if we could, prefer it not happen. But still, in that moment, we do have a choice. We have to decide for ourselves, what being cut off means.

For some their instant reaction is rage and loudly yell in their car, "You jerk. You could have killed me." Others might respond with a shrug and wonder about people's lack of awareness. "Probably texting," they might think. A few might even feel concerned about their hurriedness. Maybe they are late for an important meeting or rushing to an emergency and not paying attention.

In each instance, how we perceive the event decides our emotional state. If we respond with anger, it is because we see ourselves as vulnerable and able to be hurt. We may consider it an insult and complete disregard for our well-being. Deep down, we may question our own worthiness and this other driver reinforces that belief.

But, if instead, we respond with compassion, or understanding, we see ourselves as powerful, worthy beings.

How we feel about events outside us, is always how we feel about ourselves. We cannot lay blame on other people, because our feelings are based on our beliefs and not their actions.

Yes, we are accountable for our behavior and how we treat each other. There is no justification for behaving badly, simply because perception is a choice. In truth, what we do to others, we first do to our ourselves.

If we regard others with indifference, it is because we have looked at our self without love. When we don't care about our own well-being, how can we care about the well-being of those around us? What we do, always reveals our self-perception.

Ultimately, we are responsible for how we judge what other people do, because, only we can decide what they do means to us.

What does it mean to be a victim?

A victim is someone who does not choose their own experience. It happens to them, whether they like it or not. A victim is not a creator, for creators always have a choice.

We cannot consciously orchestrate all the events we encounter. Most of daily life is out of our control. So how then, is it possible to be the determiner of our experience and not its victim?

The power is in the perception.

What impacts us most in life? Is it events, or how we feel about them? Getting cut off is hardly remembered later on we can go on with the rest of our life unaffected. But anger is not so easily left behind. We carry it with us the whole day and it overshadows everything we do, until we choose to let it go.

The challenge we face, is our willingness to see things differently, when our perception brings us unhappiness or pain. We have to learn to put aside judgment for peace.

A creator has to take responsibility for their perceptions, a victim does not. Oftentimes, that puts us in the position of making changes and that does not come without resistance. A victim, however, doesn't have to do anything because they are not the cause.

For them, what has to get better is the outside world. But consider how hopeless a position this is. We become dependent on things we cannot control. There is no power in that, or joy. It becomes a prison of fear. Isn't it better then, to deal with our resistance to change, rather than the pain of being unable to make change?

**I am not a victim,
but a Creator of my experience.**

In this basic Truth, is all the rest. How sadly are we taught differently. If we can decide how we interpret life events and circumstances, then no matter what we encounter, there is hope for happiness. Isn't this what our dreams are really all about? Enjoying life? Living to the fullest? Wouldn't you say, all we do is our attempt to be happy. Here then is the doorway.

Jesus said, if someone strikes you, turn the other cheek. But he meant this figuratively, not literally. He was not asking to let someone smack us around and do nothing about it.

Really, what he meant was - You have the ability to decide what something means. We have such power, we can encounter the most egregious act against us and still choose how we will experience it. By refusing to accept another's purpose as our own, we decide our own fate. Is this not the essence of freedom?

**We are responsible for what we see.
This is the truth that sets us free.**

Having come this far, any reasonable person will ask, if we are the Creator of our experience, then why do bad things happen to us? Because no one in their right mind would choose their own destruction.

The answer is simple, though difficult to accept. We do not choose bad things. Rather, we allow for them when we foster and maintain negative thoughts and beliefs.

When we learn how to let go of fear and guilt, our belief in being powerless, actions not seen before, suddenly seem possible. In discovering our own inner strength, we then are able to shape events and alter circumstances.

The Universe is not against us. But there are many difficulties we encounter, without our consent. Some physical events are not consciously chosen but seem to arise from the chaos of the world or the evil intent of another.

A young woman jogging in the park, just wants to get healthy and not attacked and murdered. An old woman crossing the street, is eager to get home, not run over by a drunk driver. A teenager taking a selfie wants approval from her friends, not fall off a ledge.

Very few do things for the purpose of getting hurt or injured. They are not motivated by self-destructiveness. It is hard to imagine a young innocent child getting cancer from having negative thoughts. So, there is another aspect of life we must consider, to help us understand what seems unexplainable.

There are deeper currents of our experience that cannot be fathomed at first glance. It is only through greater wisdom, that what is incomprehensible through the lens of limited human life, is made clear.

Decisions are made at another level of Beingness, where knowledge is more expansive but makes no sense to the physical self. Yet, we bear the burden of that choice. So, in that regard, we can feel like a victim of our own greater reality.

Oftentimes, there is no justice in the world according to the rules we make. We decide life must be a certain way and when it is not, we are disillusioned. But we did not set the Earth on its course or breathe Life into all that lives. We are given the freedom of decision and this is the only power we need to gain a joyful, peace-filled existence.

Sometimes, we walk a path that ends at a cliff
with no way over.
Should we then, curse our fate
and turn back in defeat?
Maybe worse, stumble on off the edge
and perish in the abyss below.
Or, perhaps, we can set aside what we think is possible
and learn to fly instead..

SECTION TWO

Opening the door to understanding

All those who live, seek for happiness. Even the darkest mind despairs over the darkness at some level and seeks relief. What a world it would be if more of us were joyful. Perhaps, this is the biggest dilemma of our lives, our nation, our planet - the simple fact most of us are not.

Whenever we are happy, in that moment we are completely fulfilled. There is nothing greater or more to achieve. The problem for us though is, contentment is not a constant state. It ebbs and flows, rises and falls, it comes and goes. So, it seems real lasting joy is impossible to achieve and we are fated to always be seeking for something we cannot attain.

Happiness is having what we will. Most of us, however, equate getting what we want with material gain. If we asked anyone, what would make you happy, most answers would be related to money and having an abundance of it. It is believed by many that solves all problems.

If only I had more, I wouldn't have fear or guilt, concerns or worries. I could quit the job I hate, with the people I don't like and be free to do whatever I please. That would be paradise.

Some are concerned with emotional needs and wants. I'd be happier if I had better friends. Or perhaps, a certain look, a certain family, a certain something. The list goes on according to the individual. Though, no matter what it is, we never seem to get enough and always feel deprived.

How then can we ever be fulfilled?

There are levels of happiness and satisfaction on one does not fulfill the other. As a being of both matter and energy, each aspect of who we are has needs to be met. Oftentimes, we confuse the two and this leads us to seeking in the wrong place for the right answer; seeking outside what can only be found within.

We are very focused on physical existence and identify with the body. Because it is totally reliant on things apart from itself for survival, we think, this is also true for Inner being.

In a very real sense, the body is lacking. It cannot exist without elements from the world. The lungs are only *happy* when they have air to breathe; the stomach when it has food to digest or water to drink. It only has a sense of well-being, when it has all it needs to live. So, because of this incompleteness, we also believe, as emotional beings, we are dependent on what is outside for inner fulfillment.

A great part of being discontented comes from this misunderstanding. We are not just a physical being. We are a nonphysical mind acting, through a body. There is a difference and within that difference lies our whole journey.

Much of society is set up to make the body satisfied, not the mind. Everything we do, in some way, is directed at helping it survive more easily and comfortably, which is why our lives are so dominated by having money and getting more. Without it, we cannot meet our physical needs and therefore, because we identify our self as a body, we think, the I AM of Being needs money to survive.

There is no denying the flesh in a material world. But this is not a reason for imagining, we are what we are not. In truth, by living more in alignment with our Reality, the happier our lives become.

People are overweight because they consume more food than they need. So why do they do it? Because they believe, the comfort of eating can bring release from emotional pain.

This thinking applies to any form of addiction. We pretend we can satisfy our mind, through satisfying our body. But this never works. Nothing physical can change a non-physical condition. Cause cannot be altered by manipulating its effects. Unhappiness is not physically transformed and neither is peace achieved, through anything material.

If we can accept this fundamental Truth, we save ourselves many long years of suffering. If we attempt to use anything of a physical nature to bring us a sense of joy, we will always fail. It is only by understanding the mind and its fulfillment, that we can ever hope to find any real dependable sense of well-being.

Happiness is a state of mind, not a state of body.

What brings the mind joy?

What brings the mind joy, is the same as what brings it misery, is the same as what gives the body comfort or distress.

When our stomach is empty, we feel a sense of nausea or upset. We might even say, "I am starving to death."

For us, this state is painful. When we have nothing to eat, we suffer; when we lack water to drink, we die of thirst. Equally though, we have a sense of contentment, after eating until we are full.

Physical existence is very basic and we are all proficient at meeting our bodily needs. But our mental existence is not so easily understood and mastered.

Here is a paradox. The mind has no needs because it is not lacking anything. So, the real question is, what makes our nonphysical Self contented?

Ask anyone what they seek and the list is diverse and endless. There is not one thing, that meets all needs. Having money is not a panacea for life's ills, for some of the most dysfunctional people on the planet are wealthy. Likewise, many of the happiest beings on Earth, have not much in the way of material fortune.

Being healthy makes us happy, but miserable people are not always sick and some sick people live in peace. For others, having a family and friends brings them joy. But then, there are those who ask, "Have you seen my family?" pointing with disdain.

It becomes obvious, the dilemma we face when talking about what makes us happy is, there is no single answer that fits all people. Yet, what is true, by its very definition is the same under all conditions, all the time, everywhere. So, if there is a truth to happiness, it must apply equally to everyone.

The Simple Truth of Happiness

Happiness is a state of mind and no different than any other mental state. It is caused by thoughts, that arise from beliefs about what something means.

The real truth of happiness is found,
in the meaning we give our self and our life.

If we close our hand and stick a thumb up, in our culture, that's a positive sign of something good and others might smile in response.

If we thrust our index finger into that air, we are declaring ourself number one and others could feel competitive against us.

If we make a fist and raise our middle finger, most find that insulting and get angry.

But, if we used our pinky and waved, people would be baffled and not know what to feel.

So, what is the real difference between these actions? Nothing of consequence. They're all the same thing – closing a hand and raising a finger. But each one causes a different emotional response because their content is different. Content, another word for meaning, is what we all respond to and not the form itself.

All Happiness
lies in Content

Physical form, by its very nature, is neutral and only represents what is nonphysical. In seeking to understand the nature of happiness, we have to make a clear distinction between the outer form and the inner meaning.

Everything in the world is just a symbol for something else. Words, written or spoken, are not the thoughts they reflect. Someone speaking a different language is not understood, if we don't know the meaning of the sounds they make. Hearing words doesn't cause us to feel a certain way. It is what is being said, that brings us sadness or joy.

Some meanings bring peace.

Some meanings lead to despair.

A man wearing a suit in an office, is seen as being professional and treated with respect. He feels good about himself as part of the team. The same man, in jeans and boots is disregarded as being unprofessional and feels afraid of getting reprimanded.

On a ranch, someone in a suit is considered out of place, looked on with suspicion and kept apart. While wearing jeans and boots they fit in and feel good being there, because they are warmly welcomed.

A woman wearing a tight skirt and high heels at a fashion show feels beautiful, because of all the positive attention. At a feminist rally, where everyone wears sneakers, she might be considered a symbol of male objectivism and feel badly.

For different people, the same form can have a different meaning and so, cause different feelings. It cannot be then, circumstances or events are the source of happiness, if happiness is the same for everyone.

It would seem obvious to say, if we want to be happy in life, do what is expected and don't do what is unacceptable. But that is a very limited view, based on being fulfilled by certain conditions, or in pleasing others.

It is impossible we all use the same symbolism. So, living life according to someone else's ideals only leads to failure. But what we do share, is what certain content brings and that is where Truth is found.

If we asked everyone the same question and compared all the answers, stripping away the outer layers of individual symbolism, we discover the core meaning is always the same.

Putting on a suit to go to work can't make you happy but being accepted will.

Wearing jeans on a ranch doesn't bring joy but feeling welcomed does.

Having on high heels isn't pleasing but feeling beautiful is glorious.

Running around in sneakers is not a cause for celebration but joining with others in a united stand is.

So, what do all these conditions mean, that each one, though completely different, causes the same emotional response?

In some way, in whatever circumstance, we are happy when we feel a sense of Love and unhappy when we don't.

All Happiness comes from Love and all unhappiness comes from its absence. Love is both a Truth and an Answer. Love is the Truth of Happiness and the answer to all misery.

The simple truth of happiness
is Love.

When we look at our life and whatever brings us joy, we always see it as a symbol for love, being loved or being loving.

Being popular is getting positive attention and adoration means we are loved.

Money cannot buy contentment. But for many, it is the sign of self-worth. When we think, having it means we are valuable, we feel blessed, while not having it makes us feel worthless and cursed.

What is the loving view of our Self and what is not?

Physical objects are but empty vessels that can be filled with positive or negative meaning. All positive meaning reflects love and all negative meaning reflects what is not love.

Many people say, it is their family's that bring them the greatest happiness. But what is it about a family that brings joy? It's not the cleaning up and doing laundry, working at a job to support them, not the children fighting or the messy house they leave. It is none of these things. It is the Love we have for them and their Love for us.

There is no other answer in life except this one. Everything we think will make us happy but represents Love.

Love and only Love makes us happy.
All else brings misery.

The Path to Love

When we have what we Love we are happiest. When we don't, we are miserable. How simple is that to understand and so easy to achieve. Oh? Not so easy to have what we love? Or perhaps, the difficulty is in having only what we love.

If our lives were filled with just the things and people we cared about, there is no doubt we would always be joyful. Isn't that Heaven? But, in this world, that is never true.

Our day-to-day existence is populated with things we want and things we don't, people we adore and some we dislike, conditions we enjoy and those we despise.

Here is the challenge all humans face – to be truly happy, we must live a life full of love and forgive everything else that is not.

For many of us though, love is a mystery. We have no idea why we love what we love, or whom we love. We don't know what brings it closer or pushes it away. Too often, it is romanticized and imagined to be found only in intimate relationships. Being in love, is some form more special than the rest. We don't say, we're in love with our mother, or children. There is a love for this and that and there seems no fundamental Love that is inclusive of everyone and everything.

Our society is filled with misconceptions and illusions about what Love really is. No wonder happiness is so elusive, when it depends on what is undependable and difficult to find. To gain Love and keep it, we must understand it. To understand it, we must know its Truth.

The First Great Truth of Love

Love is a state of mind
and being a state of mind follows the laws of Mind.

We are used to our minds being in constant flux. We do not hold onto thoughts for very long and so, it seems our thinking is unstable. Since feelings arise from perceptions, we view our experience as unreliable. If Love is in the mind, it appears to be a phantom that comes and goes without reason. It's not surprising then, we try to place it somewhere else.

It is common to equate Love with the heart. It seems more trustworthy, if it arises from a place that doesn't change; being part of the physical world, it doesn't vacillate, but beats constant in its gentle rhythm.

But honestly, the heart has nothing to do with emotion. Truth is not sentimental, thinking creates all emotional states of being and nothing else.

Our state of mind is determined by our thoughts
and not our circumstances.
Love being a state of mind follows our thinking.

The answer to this inconsistency is not to do what cannot be done, but rather think only thoughts that inspire Love. Then, our entire experience will be one of peace and happiness.

Practically though, how many can achieve this glorious state of being? We all have the potential, but few have the willingness. Anyone can climb a mountain, but only those with fortitude reach the peak.

The real question we must ask ourselves is, how can our thinking be more consistently loving?

How we work is not mysterious. What makes anything a mystery is lack of attention. When we turn our focus onto seeking an answer, the truth is suddenly revealed. Why do we think thoughts that are loving and those that are not? The answer lies within our belief system.

What is a loving thought and what is not? There are characteristics to each.

I think you are a wonderful person. I consider you great. I want you to succeed in everything you do are loving thoughts.

You are a terrible person. You are a loser. I hope you fail miserably. These are unloving.

There are an infinite number of thoughts that are considered loving and as many that are not. We cannot control our thinking and so, to examine each idea we have and decide which are worth keeping and those letting go, is an impossible task. Rather, to understand what causes a loving thought, we have to look deeper to the question, what is Love?

What is Love?

Love is a good feeling. It is happiness, peace, and warmth. Love can be described in innumerable ways. Love is kind, patient, and generous. All of which are descriptions or attributes of Love. But what is Love itself?

Love is energy and like all energy is experienced in the mind as feeling and emotion.

Love is a Vibration of Mind.

This pattern called Love, follows the same laws of creation as any other feeling. What we think we feel.

Love comes from our perception about something or someone. And what is the core of any idea, but its meaning. Love therefore, arises from content.

Love is inspired by meaning.

In our world of form and process, nothing has absolute definition and so, there is no circumstance or person, that always inspires love. Seeking for Love where it cannot be found, is a fruitless search. But, like happiness, even though there are innumerable symbols for what makes us happy, the fundamental reason is the same.

If all love arises for the same source, what perception then, brings forth Love?

What do we love? We love our children and spouse. We love sports, money, cars. People love shopping or cooking, exercising, and traveling. But this kind of love is not always constant.

Many love their families, but every parent knows, there are moments when you despise your children and certainly hate your spouse. Some love to shop, but their partner doesn't love the bill and who loves to cook all the time? Even chefs need a vacation.

But, the one thing rarely said is, we hate money. When it comes to money, it is only hated in its absence. Is there anyone so miserable with wealth, they have to give it all away to be happy? Not on this planet.

Here is an interesting clue to the meaning of Love. All these things are symbols for something greater. What really is the worship of the almighty dollar?

Primarily, we need to get things and the things we get are about helping us to live. We love money, because we can have whatever we desire. We will never starve, never go cold, or get wet. We can eat in any restaurant or live in any mansion. Money is a resource to survive.

In truth, what we care about are not strips of paper or digital coins, but what it can do. It is the power to exist in our society, without it we could not function.

Here is the core idea behind everything that represents Love. It helps us to live and continue living. Whatever we love, is something that we see as bringing us Life.

Life is the meaning behind all Love.

We love our children because they are part of us. We gave them something of ourselves in their inception and sustain their existence by raising them. We keep them safe and safeguard their well-being. Isn't this why they love us? Isn't it the same for our spouse? We love them because they share our life and we share theirs; together we live.

People get divorced, because the caring has left the marriage. They have stopped being supportive of each other, in some manner.

Think about everything we love. If it is cooking, is it the of chopping of meat and vegetables, standing in front of hot stove sweating that we adore? Or are we passionate about creating something that give others nourishment, that feeds their body and their soul?

Love is what brings life.

People are avid about watching sports. But how does that make their life better? What is the value of seeing a football game, at home, on the couch?

Any sport is a competition, a symbolic battle. Each team or person seeks to defeat their opponent. But it's not the losing people cheer. It's the winning. No one loves a loser, for failing. Why? Because winning at anything, is seen as a victory over whatever seeks to defeat us.

Here is the key to unlocking the mystery of human existence. Why we love something and why we don't, is the same reason. What we love supports our will and what we hate opposes it.

Whatever makes us unhappy always appears to be threatening or endangering us. This applies not only to our physical well-being, but our mental life as well.

What is our life?

We know what our physicality is, but few fully realize, they have an emotional/mental reality just as valid, even more so.

Breathing, eating, sleeping, walking, sweating, sitting, standing, digesting, pumping blood encompasses the body's existence. Thinking, feeling, believing, dreaming, hoping, envisioning is the life of the mind.

To truly understand Love, we must recognize all its aspects, because Love is all about Life – our entire life.

The mind's existence is found in thinking and feeling what we believe and experience non-physically. At its center is the self-concept, the foundation of our entire thought system. Quite simply, we want what reinforces the vision of our self and oppose what doesn't.

If I believe I am a kind person. I will honor all those who show me kindness because it reinforces my belief in myself. But I will also despise those, who think I am not, whether through their anger or disregard, because it threatens my belief in myself.

The Life of our Mind is all about identity and who we consider ourselves to be. All those we cherish, all things we hold dear, in some way, reinforces what we believe about our Self.

Who we are is a state of mind
and so, we love what supports our thinking.

Most of us carry negative thoughts about ourselves. No one is fully convinced of their own worth and goodness. It is not enough then, to say, we only love what agrees with our thinking. Rather, true love supports the best vision of who we are, not the lowest concepts we hold.

No one loves their failures. No one loves their darkness. No one loves the wrongs they do and the hurt they bring. These are our illusions, not our Truth. But to be happy in life, we must embrace our whole self. So, we learn to forgive what we see as our worst parts, knowing when we love, we are transformed.

We only Love the best of our self,
because only that is true.

The Second Great Truth of Love

Love is not different. It is always the same.

There is not a different love for various occasions. Love is One in all circumstances and conditions. It varies in form and expression perhaps, certainly, in intensity. But at its essence, Love is always the same.

When we are happy, we feel happy. Why we are changes, but the feeling of happiness does not. So, would Love be any different, if both are energy? When we Love, we feel it completely, no matter what the reason.

Some will say the love we have for our favorite food and our children are not the same. But this is not the Truth.

I enjoy vegetables for how they taste and what they achieve. I find them delicious and eating them brings me a sense of pleasure. They feed and support the life of my body, so I love vegetables.

I love my children for many reasons. Most importantly, they share my life and I share theirs. We support each other's emotional existence and are devoted to one another.

But there really is no difference in my love of brussels sprouts and for my kids, except to the degree each sustains my life and supports my self-identity.

I care about my daughters with a deep intensity because our lives are so interconnected. They are part of me and I of them and who we are together is who I am.

Vegetables I enjoy but can live without. I am not a vegetarian and it's not an integral part of my self-image. So, my desire for them is not as intense. If I were though, I would be obsessed with having them.

For most of us, caring about another person, is the greatest expression of all and certainly not comparable to our favorite pair of shoes. But this is not the way the mind works and it is the mind where Love is experienced.

There was a man, whose career was his passion. He had two wonderful sons and a wife who adored him. But if he had a choice between taking his kids for a bike ride or watching the stock market he would choose the ticker tape. He was so engrossed in work, over time, he became alienated from his family and got divorced.

If the love of family were the ultimate Love, why then would someone forsake that to pursue wealth? The answer is this: It's all relative to what we value.

John grew up poor. His father worked long hours, as a slave, he felt, to a company who could take his livelihood away at any moment. What little money they had, was gained with struggle and his father always felt, supporting a family was a burden. Eventually he died in the mines, leaving his wife and children desolate.

When John got married, he promised himself not to suffer the same fate. So, he worked constantly, because he believed that was his salvation.

It became clear, what he loved about money was, it brought him a sense of power. He was the happiest when closing a deal, not celebrating a birthday, which he considered an expense and not a profit.

Sadly, he lost sight of the value of his family and for him, his survival was more about meeting his own needs, then the needs of others.

But whether our perception is considered socially right or wrong, is irrelevant. How we perceive the world, results in our experience and Love is not excluded from that process.

The Mind does not decide if we should love our children more than dollars. It follows its own nature, which says, we experience energy in accord with our beliefs. Love is always inspired by Life and that which brings Life. If we believe that is gained and supported by money and not having a family, we will Love money more.

This may give the impression Love is somehow less real. We think it should be more stable and constant; always come from the heart and have an absolute quality. It doesn't seem right, we can cherish money more than human life. But for some, material wealth is of greater value and the feelings they have are just as valid, regardless of the object of their affection. Energy is not personal and does not judge or discriminate.

Those with lesser motives do not feel love any less,
than those with more noble intent.

While Love does not change in any circumstance, it does differ in substance and depth according to our thinking. Love is a light. Light is always the same, but its radiance can vary.

There is a woman who lived in a very affluent town. She would drive her kids to school in an older model minivan. In the pickup in line, she'd see all the other mothers in their expensive SUVs waiting for their children. She loved being a mom like them but dreamed about the life they lived. At school functions, she would try to join in the conversations, but cliques aren't welcoming to outsiders. So, she made it a vow, to one day get her own luxury car.

After years of working an extra job and saving every penny, she was able to fulfill her dreams. That day, pulling up in front of the school, was the happiest she felt in a long time. The other mothers at first perplexed, finally, gave the nod of approval. From then on, her whole life seemed to change and she was invited to the inner circle of the PTA.

She loved driving around town, going to the supermarket, to the pharmacy and always trying to get the most noticeable spot. It was her baby and she took care of it like a proud momma.

One day, her oldest daughter wanted to use the car to go to a party and show off to her friends. Her mother was extremely reluctant at first but relented after constant asking. Giving her daughter the keys, she prayed for her safety.

"Don't damage my car, "She yelled.

Later that night, the phone rang. Her daughter was in an accident.

"My baby," She cried. "Is my baby, ok?" "

"Your daughter is fine." The officer said.

"Ok." The mother said. "But how is my car?"

"Oh, its totaled."

The next few days were the darkest hours, as the mother tried to accept the loss of her beloved treasure. She could not let go of her anger at her daughter's irresponsibility, even though it was not really her fault. She felt life was over and never again, would she be happy. She lost what she loved so much.

After a week of driving around in silence, in the old minivan, her daughter finally broke into tears. "I am sorry, it was not my fault." Her mother turned in rage, ready to scream, when she suddenly realized, the car was damaged, but her daughter was fine. "Thank God." Aside from some emotional trauma, she walked away unscathed.

In that moment, all the love she had been holding back, came flooding in and she started sobbing, imagining how she'd feel if her daughter had been hurt instead. Truly, she thought, if that happened, she couldn't go on living.

Love and Life are interdependent. Where there is Life there is Love. Where there is Love there is Life and what we see ourselves connected to, we will cherish with undying devotion.

The mother adored the car because she saw it as adding to her esteem and brought the admiration of her peers. It validated the view of herself as a worthy person and that made her happy. But, when she recognized her daughter as the real treasure, the car became meaningless.

A car can be replaced, a child cannot. For her, driving in luxury was a status symbol that supported the life of her ego. But having a healthy child sustained the life of her soul. So, what has the greater importance? An idea of what we are to others, or the truth of who we are to our self?

The illusion of Love

If Love is based on the meaning we give, what happens when that meaning is not true?

Imagine we meet someone and fall madly in love. They have all the qualities we've been looking for in a mate - attractive, fit and generous. We are swept off our feet. After dating for a short time, we decide to get married and start planning our life together. We are so happy, we can't contain our Self.

But then one day, as we are moving some boxes of their personal belongings, we discover love letters from another person. Suddenly, it is revealed, they were having an affair. In that one instant, all the deep caring we thought we had, evaporates and turns into hate and anger.

This love was based on illusions and when the lie was uncovered, all the good feelings there a moment before, disappeared without a trace. So, the question is, how real could this have been, that it vanished so quickly and was replaced with its opposite?

Love that is based on Truth is real.

Love based on illusion is false.

Feelings can be false when they are founded on what is not true. The experience is the same. We feel the emotional intensity of our thoughts. But they only last as long as we continue to believe in them.

Such an event proves, we are the creator of our reality and what we think we feel. Even when, what we believe is not true, still our emotions are no less powerful.

This form of love though, is conditional and what is based on characteristics and traits has shallow roots; having been planted in ground that shifts and moves it is unreliable.

Those who lay foundations on sand, risk their lives when a tidal wave comes. But houses anchored on bedrock can withstand any storm.

Love that is built on Truth is unconditional and does not change when conditions change. Only in this sense, we say it is real. Illusions are no less powerful than Truth in their effects. But the hallmark of reality is, being always the same, under all circumstances.

The Third Great Truth of Love

Love is not special

In our society, it's accepted, what is ordinary has little value. Why is gold worth so much? Because of its shiny color? Other metals, such as copper are as colorful, but we don't make pennies out of gold. Is it because it does not rust? Stainless steel doesn't either, but no one puts a diamond in a chrome setting. Or perhaps it has excellent electrical properties?

No. What gives gold importance is scarcity. For us, the less of something there is, the more valuable it appears to be and what there is an abundance of, is considered too commonplace to merit any real attention.

If everybody could sing beautifully or act well or perform athletic feats, we would not have such a celebrity driven culture, since fame is founded on abilities only a few possess. Anything everyone can do, is not considered special and because it is ordinary, it is not celebrated or held in high regard.

Our whole society's concept of value is founded on lack. If there is a huge supply of a product, its cheap. If there is a shortage it costs more.

If there is only one of something, how deeply is it treasured? Perhaps, that depends on what it is. If rarity alone were the basis of specialness, then those one-in-a-million medical conditions would be featured in a magazine. Or the rare person struck by lightning who lived, would be given an award. But no one wants either one. So, it is the desire for something that increases it worth.

We all want to drink water. But, because it is so plentiful and anyone can have it, a bottle costs pennies compared to champagne; most restaurants give it away for free. In a desert though, it may be priceless.

For something to be special, it has to be considered valuable and scarce; having the quality of desirability, but also something only the elite can have. The rarest gems, the most precious metals and the greatest prized possession all share these traits. Specialness is considered the seal of worth. The more distinct it is, the more it is coveted.

What does it mean to value something?

Something valued is something Loved.
We only love what we value.

Too often, we believe, we can only love what is special. This is true for objects, as well as people. In our search for love, aren't we looking for that special someone? No one says they're seeking the ordinary. But how is anyone so different from the billions of other people in the world? Why do we love one person over another?

In our society, we separate ourselves into categories and place a value on each one. Beautiful is something to love and ugly is despised. Strong is admirable and weak pitiful. Tall is stately and short is lacking. Thin is in and fat is out. Rich is required and poor is a deal breaker. It's endless.

Many personal ads ask for tall, dark and handsome, few want short, pale and ugly. Most men want a model wife, but who desires that overweight spinster? But is this what Love is really about?

It is, if Love is limited. I will adore you, if you meet these conditions, look a certain way or, have a high position. I will cherish you deeply if you are wealthy. Or maybe, what I really care about, is your money. You can come along, if you bring your wallet.

Love based on specialness is conditional and if those conditions are gone, the feelings go as well. How more obvious is this, than the world of celebrity, where one day you are the hottest thing and the next day, old news? Were you ever really glorious if the glory fades?

This is not Love, but a shabby imitator, whose threads unravel and tear over time. The warmth it once gave, does not endure and we are left abandoned to shiver in the cold of loneliness.

True Love is Unconditional

The Love that comes from Truth, is not capricious. It does not alter from moment to moment, come and go like the wind, or rise and fall like the sun. It is always present and unending, for Truth is only true if it is constant.

If we love someone, because of something they've done, that is not unconditional. If our child comes home with an A on a school report and we say how proud we are, is it because of the grade or because of who they are? Would we care for them any less if they got a C?

Hopefully, we support their wellbeing, regardless of their accomplishments or behavior. Unless we lack understanding of what being loving means, then our love swings back and forth from right to wrong and back again; never steady, never to be counted on when needed.

What is the foundation of all Love? Is it not Life? To be someone special, we must possess a quality others lack. But, consider if this is reality, that some have a greater existence than everyone else.

It is true, in the world, lifestyles vary considerably. A billionaire and an office clerk live different forms of life. One may sleep in a mansion on the ocean, another in a walk-up downtown. A wealthy person might have a private jet and ride in limousines. An ordinary person takes cabs or rides the subway to work.

But in Truth, they have the same fundamental existence. They share a common motivation and follow the same laws of mind; both arise from the wellspring of shared Being. Each are born of flesh, grow to adults, eat and breathe, sometimes laugh, and sometimes cry along the way. They get sick, they heal, they age and die. They come from within and quietly return, leaving their footprints on the paths they tread and neither one is forgotten by those they loved.

No one is special, but each has value.
Life is common, but forever sacred.
Love is not for some but belongs to all.

There is absolutely no difference between the joy of a billionaire and the joy of a clerk. It is all one energy. It is a great falsehood to pretend, some have a superior self by virtue of the possessions they hold.

Life does not have to be more, for us to be happy. People dream of being rich and famous, but it is not necessary for peace and happiness. Rather, it's a hidden obstacle, because it is not fact, but a storied myth. When we strive to make Life into something it can never be, we fail and suffer out of allegiance to mistaken dreams.

Only what is true is real, everything else is illusion.
Idols are not gods and statues who pose, don't live.
Stars only shine in darkness.
Love is the true Light of Heaven

Here, Life is everywhere. It grows in the deepest valley covered in shadows and on the highest mountain bathed in sunlight. It rests on manicured lawns of gated homes, on concrete stoops in dirty slums. It flourishes in the limelight and under an oil lamp. It can sit on the most magnificent throne. But, its greatest reign, is often found in the simplest existence.

In one breath Life is common, in another extraordinary, beyond comprehension. Where in all the Universe is there such Grace and Beauty as on the Earth? That we live, that we can Love and be Loved, is enough for us to have a life worth living.

The Fourth Great Truth of Love

To have Love, we must give Love

In our world, to have anything, we believe we must get it from outside our self. We are so focused on physical existence, we assume this applies to our inner life as well. The body is not self-sustaining and cannot survive without external nourishment. The mind, however, is Energy and needs nothing but itself to live.

It's common to think, to have love, someone must love us. It doesn't make sense to say, to have love, give it. How can we give what we don't have? If we had it, we wouldn't be seeking it. But love is not physical and follows non-physical laws, not material rules.

What does it really mean to have Love, we must give Love?

It means this: no matter how lovingly others treat us, we may still feel unloved; no matter how miserably we are abused, we can still be at peace.

How we feel is a result of our thinking and not caused by our environment. For us to feel love, we have to see everything with love. Giving Love is literally, thinking loving thoughts, or having loving beliefs.

Perception is the meaning we ascribe to circumstances and events. If we perceive the world through ideas of Love, no matter what is happening, we are fulfilled.

In the same manner, if we perceive the world without love, no matter how comfortable our surroundings, how loud the applause we receive, we will not be happy or at peace.

In the realm of Mind, we only have what we create. It cannot be given to us, for such is our freedom. There is no more important statement than this in understanding our self.

Here we come face to face with the world. There are accepted meanings we all agree on. They are not absolute. But that we share them, they take on the appearance of Truth.

Walking up to someone and slapping them in the face is not perceived as loving, But, kissing them on the cheek is a sign of respect. Yet, it does not matter what the action is. Sometimes, slapping them in the face when they've taken pills, is more caring than kissing them on the cheek in betrayal. It's all in the meaning and all meaning is in the mind.

To be filled with Love we must follow the laws of emotion, not the rules of convention.

It often seems, we only have self-worth when others treat us kindly and feel worthless when treated poorly. This, we believe as a culture. But what happens when others don't regard us the way we want to be regarded? Are we no longer a creator, but a victim of their actions instead?

We all want to be cherished, respected and adored. In all things, that is what we strive for and desire most in Life. When it is said, Love comes from within and shines out, this is literally true. What we receive, may inspire us to give in return. But we are never empty vessels, filled by the emotions of others.

We are Beings of Energy and Energy can manifest itself as Light. Love is a light because it is an Energy. We can never be cast into darkness, because of what we are. But we can shut our eyes to Truth and think we are blind. We are always surrounded by the Light of Love but cannot know that unless it flows through us into the world.

When we feel disregard, we have judged someone or something as unworthy, even if that someone is our self. We cannot have what we don't give; feel what we don't think or believe.

We cannot have love inside, when we are unloving to those outside.

Here is a seeming paradox of cause and effect. What we give we receive. When we give love, others must respond with love in return. If we are not receiving love, then we are not giving it. Though, this can easily be misunderstood when we think about form and not content.

In life, when we feel mistreated, it is often because we have decided someone else's behavior is abusive. So, we assume feeling badly is a result of their actions. But Energy is not created this way. Our unhappy feelings, come from our perception of them and not their lack of love.

For a moment, put aside logic and social norms and look as a Creator not a victim.

It's really not getting slapped that causes upset. It's that we have judged being attacked as degrading. Physically it can sting, but that pain passes. Emotionally though, we see it as being disrespected and that is the real reason we suffer.

A physical act has no inherent meaning. We allow that behavior to affect us, when we decide, to see ourselves as vulnerable and demeaned. We perceive each other through the eyes of self-perception. If we feel beaten down, it is because we have looked within and seen ourselves capable of being hurt.

Yes, there is physical trauma. But no person, certain of their invulnerability, would ever think the actions of others creates their inner state of being.

To have love, we give love. But what we give others, we first give ourselves. We don't condone bad behavior, when we take responsibility for our perceptions. We take back our power.

Abusers will suffer the judgment of their own thought system. They condemn themselves to misery, each time they look upon anyone without love. For, they have first looked within and found themselves lacking and it is only from that void of unworthiness they attack the world. They are not in their right mind, having lost faith in the rightness of their own being.

We will suffer at the hands of others, as long as we continue to believe we can. The irony is, to be happy in life, we are the ones to make ourselves happy, to be at peace we have to be peacemakers, to be loved, we have to be loving. Regardless of what someone does, it is how we respond to them that matters most. Am I who you make of me? Or am I what I decide? Accept not their tyranny and you are free.

Love cannot be taken from us if we give it,
for what we give we receive.

A long time ago, there lived a man who walked the barren landscapes of his country, bringing healing to many. In his short life, he did great works, preaching wonderful news to all who would listen.

He was much beloved by his followers, but despised by a powerful group, who felt his message of hope threatened their authority. So, they found a way to have him arrested for crimes he did not commit, tried and sentenced.

Anyone, so wrongfully convicted, would be outraged at the injustice. Yet, he walked the road to death, in the surety of his own innocence, not as a victim of their madness, but as a Teacher of the Truth.

The final lesson he taught the world was, it matters not what our circumstances are, nor what others think about them. It matters only what we think about ourselves, that creates our emotional state.

In his mind, he did not suffer, being filled with compassion for those who sought his destruction. He was not insane, but the Master of his fate. He perceived their actions in the Light of Truth and because he chose to see them with Love, he was filled with peace, not anger.

There is no more powerful demonstration that shows, our perception of an event and its meaning is what determines how we feel. Love can be found in any situation where it seems not to be, by simply giving it.

To have Love, give love

and learn you are Love.

For we can only give of our self

and we learn what we are

by what we give.

The Fifth Great Truth of Love

Love makes all things One

Love is a feeling and like all emotions, is an energy. Energy is power that produces effects. We can say, Love is a force that does something.

Anger is an energy that attacks but does not cradle a newborn.

Fear paralyzes and cannot bravely walk a tightrope.

Peace is an energy which pacifies and creates harmony.

Different forms of energy inspire certain actions, for inherent in each one is a purpose, to obtain an objective of the mind.

If our desire is to comfort a crying baby, we don't grab them in anger and shake back and forth. We hold them calmly and rock from side to side.

If our aim is to win a battle, we don't meekly wave a white flag in surrender, but proudly raise our colors and start shooting.

When we perceive the world, first there is a goal. Then, there are the thoughts which create the feelings that lead to action.

Inherent in all energy,
there is a purpose, direction and will.

What is the purpose of Love?

What does the mind seek to achieve? If we see what it does, we understand its motivation. People don't run away when we offer them love. They don't seek our demise, when supporting their well-being. We are not mocked, expressing admiration. What people do is come closer, step into to hear our words, reach out a hand and touch ours, embrace us warmly with great affection.

Love does not repel but attracts. It brings us together and joins us as one. It is obvious then, the intention of Love is Oneness.

Love makes all things One

What does it mean to be One?

We normally think, one of something is being single and apart from everything else. Or, to make things one, we assume means, putting them together.

In the beginning of the Universe, a single field of energy, exploded outward into many separate elements. It can never be what it was, so is it still One? All the galaxies and stars and planetary systems are speeding away from each other. Is that Oneness?

I have one pillow on my bed. I see it is made of fabric and stuffing. It's not really one thing but two. As we look closer, we discover, the cover is really numerous threads of woven cotton. Looking deeper still, there is an endlessness to the little parts of everything. Even the smallest atom is composed of smaller particles. The Truth is, there is no such thing as an individual object. All physical things are a composite.

To be at one with something means that we are part of its existence and share its life.

What we are one with affects us and we affect it. What we are separate from, we have no connection to, or bearing on. The opposite of Oneness is separation, having an existence apart from everything else.

In material terms, there is no absolute state of Oneness. There is a relative togetherness. Atoms can bond, forming molecules that build larger structures, but eventually they split apart. Cells unite and create organs of a more complex body, though, that too ends in decay.

We wake up every morning in human bodies, having our own individual needs and concerns. Our physical being has an independent life. We intermingle with each other, but there is never a true joining we can call being at One.

Oneness cannot be a physical state.

So how then does Love join us and make us One? It does not unite on the bodily level but energetically and like all mental experience, is a state of mind.

Oneness is a state of mind.

All nonphysical experience, regardless of what it is, follows the laws of mind. What we think we feel. What we give we receive. All emotions serve a purpose. Love is attraction, pulling all things and making them One. It is sharing One life and One existence, not physically but emotionally and mentally.

Love is the emotion of Oneness.
Oneness is the state of Love.

When we Love someone, our strongest desire is to be with them always; falling in love, we want to make a life and a family. Love is what binds us, as energy.

Love is spiritual gravity,
holding the Universe together.

The Sixth Great Truth of Love

Love is a sharing of Life

Love and Life are inseparable. Where one is, the other must be. Love is Energy, as is Life. But we don't consider electricity alive, even though it is power. So, it must be more than just force.

In the physical world, what is alive is animated, such as plants that grow and bloom, animals that graze and hunt, human beings who build civilizations. Things without life are inanimate objects, like rocks, cars, water and even the sun.

All matter is composed of the same primary particles. Our bodies have similar elements as the Earth. It cannot be then, what lives is fundamentally unlike what does not. The essential difference between the two is, one does something purposefully, while the other simply exists.

A rock is not considered living, because it doesn't do anything of its own volition. It can't decide to roll around. If it did, we'd call it alive. So, having life means having a will.

Life is the energy of action. But there is also purpose behind that action, a consciousness that makes decisions. What is sentient, has awareness of itself as existing. Otherwise, it couldn't intentionally act and what is the most basic motivation there is? But to live and continue living.

Life, though very complex in form, is simply driven. It has but two motivations: the will to live and sustain one's existence and to grow and expand that existence. Everything we do or want arises from one or the other.

What is the role of Love in our will to live?

The answer is quite obvious. Love is the energy of attraction, the drawing together of things in a common bond. If we consider how we survive on Earth, or have ever survived, it is apparent we live best in cooperation, rather than opposition.

When we plant a seed in the ground, we don't make it to grow. Who wills the sky to form clouds and create rain? Even though we raise livestock for food and trawl the oceans, we can't force chickens to lay eggs or fish to spawn.

Without all other living things fulfilling their own purposes, we could not survive. We may think we are in competition with each other and in a limited sense this is true. But, in a broader sense it is not.

We cannot live in this world, without everyone else who lives in this world, we are that interdependent. Why do we build cities and towns? Why has mankind always flourished within some group structure? Because nothing can exist on its own. Everything we have comes from someone else.

When we get up in the morning, we brush our teeth. There is nobody there helping us, we can do it our self. But where did that toothbrush come from? We bought it in store perhaps, though it had to be there for us to buy and someone else had to make it in a factory. It is the same for the toothpaste.

Where did the water I use to rinse my mouth come from? Where does it go and what happens to it? There is an endlessness to the interconnectedness of everything. We can't even brush our teeth in the morning, without the contribution of thousands of other people. We are individuals, but still completely dependent on each other to survive.

It would be wonderful to say we do things out of love for others. But this is not obviously true. People work in factories to make money, not help in the fight against tooth decay.

Why does Mary toil every day, all day long, at some menial job that offers few rewards? She does not do it out of hate or anger, though she may go to work angry, to a job she hates.

She does it out of love – the love of her own life and for the survival of those she cares about. In the deepest sense, we could not go on, day after day, if we did not have this greater motivation.

Why do people want to love and be loved?

When we Love someone, we join with them and they share our life. Isn't it true, who you care about, you want to have all they need to live and grow? And who cares for you, seeks for your constant well-being. Is this not what being together means? Each person supporting and sustaining the existence of the other?

Fundamentally, people want to be loved, because we recognize, it is easier to journey with friends, then carry burdens alone. We want to love others, so we can expand the reach of our existence and be more than who we are, by our self. See how love fulfills our will?

In the will to live, is the Love of our self
In the will to grow is the Love of others.

Love is all about the sharing of life. It brings joy because it reinforces our existence. Happiness is having what we will, which is our existence protected.

This joining though, goes beyond the physical. Love is more than just securing the body's needs. It is also sustaining the mind.

Our nonphysical Beingness is founded in thinking; integral to that is our beliefs, whose core is the self-concept. The sharing of life includes our thoughts and the vision of who we are.

When others support these, we feel sustained. When they doubt or question them, we feel insecure.

Ideas and beliefs are strengthened
through sharing

Love gives our ideas power and strengthens them in our minds. Since they are part of our life, when others acknowledge and accept them, our Self expands. Does this not fulfill our will?

Life is a sharing of Love, to Live we must Love.

The Seventh Great Truth of Love

Love and Fear

It is held in many spiritual traditions, that Love and fear are opposites. In the Bible, it says, "Perfect Love casts out fear," and so, where one is, the other cannot be.

What is fear?

Whenever we are afraid, we have perceived someone or something as endangering us. Fear is all about being threatened. As Love comes from what sustains our life, fear arises from the resistance to our will.

Fear is an energy and like all energy has direction and motive. It is an alarm bell; a warning signal that some perceived danger lies ahead. It appears to be a supportive energy because it seeks our protection. So, many confuse fear and love for this reason.

Fear and love are interrelated. They are outcomes of a common goal. We only fear anything, because of Love. If we did not care about something, we could not be afraid of losing it. But one sees the world in a positive light and the other, in the shadows.

Where Love desires for the best to come true, fear worries about the worst that can happen.

Both seem to share the same motivation for the continuation of our life. Where they differ though is, Love is based on Truth and fear, on illusion.

Love is the statement we are One, fear, that we separate.

We are only afraid when we feel vulnerable; when we think our will can be overthrown, by some force outside our Self. What does not share our will, we see as opposing it. But, if we cannot be opposite to something we are joined with, then we can only fear what we are separate from.

Everything we fear in life,

we see as opposing our will to live.

There is no difference between fear and separation, love and oneness. We will be afraid of anything, we have no connection with, not physically but nonphysically. If all emotion comes from perception and belief is a choice, then fear is a decision to stand apart.

So, what's the issue? Some say fear is a good thing. It keeps you safe and being secure is our goal in life. It seems, to serve the purposes of love, protecting us from harm. But the dilemma is, while it appears to have good intentions, in truth, it opposes Love's aim.

What is the goal of fear? To caution us about some impending disaster, imagined or real and ensure our well-being. How can we think, this is not what we want? Of course, it is. But we never ask ourselves the question - protect us against what? Inherent in all fear, is the belief, there is something out there, that opposes us and seeks our destruction.

All enemies are born in the perception of separation,

all friends, in the recognition of oneness.

Before there is any feeling, there is the decision how to perceive events. If the world contained absolute meaning, then interpretation is not needed. But since meaning is relative, fear must be chosen.

Are we happy when afraid? At peace being fearful? If we could select between the two, what would we choose? No one in their right mind accepts fear if they recognize it as a choice. All fear is the experience of having our will defeated and who would willingly agree to their own destruction?

Even though it seems to support our desire for life, by appearing to make us safe, fear actually opposes it. Only in Love are we truly secure, because only there, have we no enemies and everything supports our will.

We can never be happy in the safety of fear,
only in the surety of Love.

The mistake we often make, is believing there are some things that absolutely cause fear. In this thinking then, how can it possibly be avoided?

If I were standing in the middle of the street and a truck is speeding towards me, it seems, we must be afraid. Yet, like every emotion, terror is a state of mind and we can elect how we perceive any situation. It is quite possible, to be completely at peace instead.

Some may argue, fear is a protective device and if we did not feel panicked, we would not jump out of the way. But this is not true, for our deepest motivation to avoid being hit and killed, is the Love of life.

Fear is a distortion of Love,
without Love it could not exist.
But without fear, Love shines undiminished.

We are far more secure in the surety of love than the safety of fear, for in love we have no enemies and in fear we have no friends.

The Eight Great Truth of Love

The resistance to Love

There is an ingrained impetus in the physical world to resist love. We feel the compelling pull towards joining and yet, the contrary push towards separation.

If only love brings joy and we all want to be happy, then we must embrace it with open arms. We should always seek to fulfill its purpose. But there is within each of us, part of our self that holds back and resists oneness.

No one alive seeks misery, for all despair is self-defeating and we cannot oppose our own self will. But, while we believe we are just a physical being, separate to and existing apart from all others, we will oppose the expansive movement of Love outward.

For many of us who want to feel safe in life, Love seems to threaten our defenses, break down our barriers and walls and lets others in. It rushes out to meet whoever is before us and embrace them as one. But, if we are sitting on the parapet of our little castle, surrounded by a moat, this doesn't seem very appealing. In fact, it's the worst thing we can imagine.

This great misperception is the result of identifying ourselves as a body. Human existence is limited and what life we have, we seem to lose by sharing. If our fundamental will is to live and grow, then it can seem Love works against us.

This is an unfortunate consequence of materiality, where what we give away, we no longer own. We believe if we love others too much, they have more than we do and so, we make our giving conditional to receiving. I will love you, only if you love me and that balances the scales.

In this world, few share unconditionally. Yet, if we love on condition, we are not being true; our peace becomes tempered and our happiness inconsistent.

The resistance to Love comes from a lack of understanding non-physical nature. When energy is extended it is strengthened not weakened. It becomes greater not less.

On Christmas Eve, in a Church somewhere, a gathering is held to celebrate a birth. Towards the end of the service, the lights are dimmed and a large candle on the altar is lit, for all the congregation to see. It shines in the darkness alone, as a soft hymn is sung.

But then, smaller candles are brought up to touch the fire and they too start burning. At each aisle, a hand is extended out and that flame is passed to everyone seated together. Row by row, the glow gets brighter, until the whole Church is filled with Light and those hushed voices become a chorus, singing Hallelujah, Hallelujah, praise to Love and Life.

The One candle still burns as bright, but in the sharing does its Light shine greater still.

When love is shared,
its light only grows brighter.

The Ninth Great Truth of Love

Love is the true motivation of All

This is hard to imagine as being true in our world of war and violence, terrorism and evil deeds. Yet it is, nevertheless.

What is motivation?

Motivation is the desire to achieve something. No action exists without some impetus behind it. There is a reason for everything we do, an implicit goal.

Why do we get up in the morning? Brush our teeth, eat breakfast and go to work? Why do we get married or invest in stocks and bonds?

All these are related to our survival, our living and continuing to live. Every decision we make, no matter how complex or simple the form, always begins with the intention to support our existence. Since Love is the desire to live, we can say, fundamentally, Love is our primary motivation.

The truth is, whatever we do,
we do because we love ourselves.

Many will disagree with this statement, on many levels. Surely, someone who drinks or eats too much doesn't do it because it supports their well-being. Someone who jumps out a window in despair isn't motivated by self-caring. A terrorist who blows up a building with innocent people inside, isn't looking for a happy life.

Love we know, makes all things one. It doesn't attack, doesn't destroy but seeks for Life. How then, is its possible, love is the motivating force behind all evil deeds?

The mind is the creator of energy and energy is the power that make decisions and formulates actions. This never changes, regardless of what is done. Its only goal is to extend itself and continue expanding.

However, when we see ourselves as separate, individual beings whose life has no relationship to any other life, then our perception gets distorted and our actions become destructive.

In all unloving deeds,
there is Love that is distorted.

A record player can give voice to the most beautiful piece of music ever written. But, if it suddenly malfunctions and speeds up, what is heard is painfully shrill and loud. In its true state the music was glorious, when it was altered, it became a nightmare.

When we drink or eat too much it's not because we hate ourselves. But rather, are looking for a way to feel better. When a terrorist plants a bomb, he thinks by destroying his enemies, it will lead to a glorious life. The issue is not our motivations. The real problem is with our thinking.

We all begin with the desire to live and be happy. This is our primary purpose. We fail to achieve that goal however, by using means that does not bring the end we seek.

Someone who harms themselves or another is trying to achieve what cannot be attained. It is not possible to get love through hate or find joining through attack.

But in their distorted thinking, they fail to realize this Truth. They believe, another is holding them down, preventing them from living their fullest existence. So, in their minds, they are victims, not creators and what do some victims do, but lash out in anger.

If we want to be happy, we must be in alignment with Truth; not use energy against its own nature and expect to reap the rewards Love brings.

Here is a question. Can we Love our Self and hate another?

The answer is no. We can only have what we give. But we can love our Self falsely and in that false light are all evil deeds born.

Harming others is all about our own survival. Wanting to survive is not a terrible thing. It is a wonderful thing. But those who attack, always do so from the belief, they are separate from and in competition with everyone else. For them, it is a self-kindness to destroy their adversaries.

But, in its natural state, Love is an energy that brings things together and makes them one. How then, is it possible to love truly and also have enemies? It is not.

Something and its opposite cannot be joined. Light and darkness are mutually exclusive. Where one is the other cannot be.

It is the law of mind - what we give others we first give our self. We can only be hateful when we feel victimized and not in command of our experience.

When we believe others determine our emotional state, we are disempowered and lack faith in our own ability to fulfill our will. Can we say this is loving? No, it is the choice to see our self without love.

In life, it is not our motives that are the failure. It is the belief, we can achieve our desires through false means. We can never be happy without the Source of all happiness, for effect and Cause are One.

The Tenth Great Truth of Love

Love is the Truth of Life

Many great spiritual masters have stated that life is One. We are all One. But what does this actually mean?

Physically, we are not one. If I eat food, it doesn't nourish your body. If you're in pain, I don't suffer. When I die, you continue living. The root problem of society is, we don't share material experience. If our lives were physically interdependent, we would never go to war or act against another.

We are so entrenched in seeing the world through our eyes, we cannot conceive of anything else. It is nearly impossible to walk down the street, with so many strangers just passing by and see any connection to them.

Sometimes, we look at our own children and feel a separation. It is the very nature of physical existence to create a sense of otherness. There are even moments when we feel disconnected from our own body.

When we are sick or in pain, it's not something wanted and there appears a gap between our will and its state. Does that sound like Oneness? At those times, when we feel it is the enemy, we inevitably wonder, "If my body and I are in opposition to each other, who feels this separation?"

Have you ever given serious thought to the question, "What am I?" Not the specifics, but the essence of who we are.

We ordinarily think of ourselves, as only being this human self. There is no way around it. We don't remember if we existed before we were born or will after we die. So, we limit our existence to a certain span of years between birth and death and call it our Life. In our day-to-day routine, there is little, if any direct evidence of something more that can be seen.

We are very much in a closed space, with no windows or view. Many have speculated on this condition and some have claimed to know what's outside the room of the world. But is it enough, to look to the past or can we find the Truth, in the present?

Today, we mostly gain knowledge through the empirical method. We believe what exists can be recognized, for what is real must show evidence of its reality. But we can never prove what does not exist, by virtue of not seeing its effects. Saying there is no outside, simply because we don't know it, is not a valid position. That is just a failure of evidence, not a lack of Truth.

Science speculates on the nature of reality all the time and puts forth many theories about the Universe. But a theory needs to be demonstrated as true, to be accepted as fact. Until then, it is just a concept.

Does one have to die though, to answer the riddle of life after death? For it seems, once you leave, you can't come back.

The basis of all religion is an answer. It has been written, Jesus died, was buried and rose from the grave, as proof of Eternity. Buddha, in his enlightenment, saw all the worlds beyond the world we know. Moses heard the Voice of God and Mohammed spoke with angels. Many great saints have all declared the reality of life after human existence. That we live and continue to live is a great comfort for those who believe in the Prophets of history.

But what is true in the past must be true today. What has been revealed before, can be discovered again. For those who want more, to see for themselves and to have that experience of knowing, there must be another way.

In the present moment, all we can see is what's in front of us; what is appearing in our life, in our view. We cannot perceive anything else. We can remember past experience, but memory can fade and becomes faith in what was, not knowledge of what is.

So, what is before us now? True, the body is here and oftentimes, it speaks the loudest of what we are. Its voice can shriek and sow doubt and if we hear only what it says, we will never be complete or happy. But there is more to our story if we listen.

Who are we really? How did we come into being? Are we here for a reason? These are such fundamental questions, they should have a ready response, but paradoxically they do not. If we accept, Truth comes in other ways then just our senses, we can find what we seek.

What we are is made manifest on a constant basis; who we are, made known in each moment. But, we must step back from established conceptions and let in a new understanding, found in a new way of knowing. There is a door that opens when we make the effort. Can we find the willingness to walk through it?

It has been said and often repeated, we are not just a body but also a mind. We are Beings of Energy. But life is not a movie and we have no powers that can move objects at a distance or create force fields. We cannot fly without wings and sparks will never, emerge from our fingertips. That is not reality, but fantasy. So, what is this energy that we really are?

It cannot be measured, but by its effects we understand what it is, by what it does.

We do not see our identity, though we know who we are, by what we give.

We don't touch our thoughts, but recognize what we believe, by how we feel.

The truth of our identity resides not in the physical self, but in our non-physical beingness. It is only realized in the energy that flows through us. Our energy is our Consciousness – the awareness of our Self.

Feelings and thoughts reveal who we think we are. But thoughts can be false and feelings illusions because they arise from beliefs, which may or may not be true.

Our truth is more fundamental. It must be what does not change but is always the same. What is within each of us that is constant, present and ever seeking expression? We are a Consciousness that has direction and motivation. What we will reflects our True Nature, for a thing can only create what is like itself.

The goal of Love is to support and expand our existence and how is this achieved, except in uniting with others in common purpose. All those who Live have the same will, for it is inherent in what Life is. Without Love there is no Life, for Life can only advance through the sharing of life.

It is our will to love our self, to continue living.
It is our will to love others,
to share and expand our being.

In the simplest way it can be said: We are an energy, in its purest state is Love. We are Love who seeks to join with others in conscious recognition of our Oneness with all other Beings. We are each part of the Whole. Though appearing separate in physical form, in non-physical reality, we share the same life, arising from the same Source.

Love is not something we have or do,
It is what we are.

Here is the most profound realization of all:

We are All One Energy
and that Oneness is Love.

This is the great Truth of Life.

SECTION THREE

Discovering the Truth

Life is a journey with many stops along the way. But sometimes it can seem to be an endless struggle and what is hard fought for and gained, only passes away and we are left to start all over again.

This seems to be the cycle of everything we do. As children, growing up, we constantly face new challenges. We go to school, advancing grades year to year, each bringing something different. Finally, after what is an eternity of studying and homework, we graduate and enter the real world.

Working at a job is a lifelong task and though we may advance in position, even change careers or perhaps start our own business, we all come to the same question, "Is this all we are meant to do?"

For many, it is a necessity, for a few a passion, but mostly, it is just about keeping the ship afloat, not having a port of call.

Many of us look to having a family for life's meaning. It seems somehow important to have children and raise them into productive adults who will continue the human race.

Of course, for us, that can be a great source of joy and love. But, when they are grown and move out to start on their own, there is an emptiness we feel of something cherished which is lost, a past that is gone and can never be recovered. True, they are still here, but it is not the same. If we believe our mission was to be a parent, what happens when that role ends?

If we are honest with ourselves, we can see how meaningless it can be. What has this lifetime of work, struggle and sacrifice actually achieved? From a material perspective, something, but is it enough?

Though we may travel for a very long time and go a great distance, if we walk in a circle, ending at the place we began, did we really go anywhere?

A journey without a destination has no purpose and what is empty of meaning has no value. Why then do we do it?

In Truth, the world is not meant to be the goal, nor is humanness the pinnacle of Beingness. If we understand its real function, then we can better appreciate the road we walk.

In physical existence, there is nowhere to go, nothing to accomplish or accumulate. But there is much to be gained and everything to see, if we seek in the right place, with true understanding.

Look not without for there is nothing there,
but look within and find the entire Universe.

There is not anything here we must do, but all things to learn. This is the true purpose of physical existence. We are meant to discover ourselves, to understand Who We Are and that can only be found by living with Love and Compassion, for that is Clarity.

Learning is living and if we are not growing, we are dying. If we would have a life of Value, then we have to look beyond the judgments of the world and begin to see things differently; not just to question everything we think we know, but be willing to be Answered by Something Greater then ourselves.

A Truth

The s/Self

Every morning we wake up and start a new day. We follow a daily routine - let the dog out, make some coffee, eat a banana. There is a usual silence. Unless, we have children and then, the house is loud and chaotic, in the mad rush to get them fed and off to school. There is no time for thinking or contemplating, only the doing.

If we slept well, we feel good, if not, we're a little cranky. We get dressed and we're outside, suddenly, confronted with the rest of the world. If we're lucky, there is not much traffic. No chance. We get stuck behind someone who doesn't know how to drive.

"Stop looking at your phone and keep up," We yell, giving them a nasty look when passing by. "What's wrong with people today?" We ask, shaking our head.

Finally arriving at the office, we sit at our desk and work begins. We do whatever it is we do, hopefully something we enjoy, not something we dread. But some people here are so difficult, we want to close off and keep our head down. Who said life is supposed to be fun anyway? The best part of the afternoon comes at 5 and we get to leave. More traffic. More stress. But an hour later, we pull safely into the driveway, relieved it's over.

Does joy greet us when we open the door? Do little feet run across the floorboards now that we are home? This house is a disaster and still more things to be done. Cooking, cleaning, yard work, chores, we can't do it by our self. Look at the pile of bills on the kitchen table. Finances are stretched thin. It never ends just another ordinary day. We wonder, "Is this all there is?"

This is the self we know, the one engaged in day-to-day activities. We make the decisions, clean up the messes, do the shopping and cut the lawn. The busyness of the world keeps us fixated on the details, we don't often see a broader view. It is oh so familiar, we think it is all that we are. But there is another part of ourselves that often goes unrecognized.

Each dawn is new opportunity to start again. We wake up to a quiet mind, like a blank canvas, we can make it what we will. Before life pulls us in, we have a choice. Do we make a list of what has to be done, or can we enjoy the sunrise? The little happiness that comes from having a clean bathroom is a simple pleasure, but it makes us feel good. We smile briefly and a small voice within, says hello. Do we respond or move on? "Hello." we say in return.

There is a frantic rush of teenagers running up and down the stairs that are behind schedule again. Don't forget your homework. Bring your lunch. It is like watching your son's football game, as he sprints down the sidelines, your daughter's dance recital as she leaps across the stage. Damn kids, always late to everything. Yet, we can see their energy in motion - barreling down the sidewalk to catch the bus in time and then turning to wave goodbye. How grateful we are, for their health and well-being and the security we give them.

Now it's our time to go. We have an important meeting and have been planning it for months. It could mean new business for our company. There is traffic, but we have time, which is good, because we need to rehearse our presentation.

We're gathered in the conference room, as the client walks in. They see our hard work and are impressed by what we've accomplished. We look around, proud of our team. We did this together. It's a good day. We won.

Finally, back at home, our spouse is cooking dinner, the kids are doing homework and the dog is already fed. We all sit down to eat. There is complaining and bickering. But there is also laughter and a sharing of good news. This is such a simple moment in our lives, but no place we rather be, no more we need to be content.

We clean the counters, put away the dishes, and see the bills that have come in the mail. So many things to pay. It seems to get tougher every year, to make ends meet. But then, reassured by the warm voice of our partner, "Don't worry, we will work it through, we always do." We're not alone and at peace in their support.

So, another day has come and gone; nothing astonishing happened. We lived the best we could. But, in brief moments, we could see something greater, founded in a deeper kindness and appreciation for Life. We don't really know what it was, but we were happier, and more patient. There was some hope we tapped into, not normally felt. We remember now, this morning we said hello. But to who or what?

When we look out, we see the reflection of our self; who we believe we are, is mirrored in the world we perceive. What events mean to us, is what we mean to events and that decides our experience.

An unimportant life is lived, not in the routines of daily living, but in the perception of having no purpose. It matters not what we do. It is Who we are doing it that makes life commonplace, or something extraordinary.

The self we know, is bound by the limits of the body. We only have so much influence, can reach so far, do so much. The focus of all our efforts is on surviving, though not really living. And if this were the extent of being human, we would be doomed to that fate, for we cannot transcend our nature. But this is not all there is and we did not Cause ourselves to be. There is a greater Reality within us all.

There is a Self we are, that transcends the world, who reaches beyond the Earth and yet, intimate as our breath. Though, often unrecognized, it is the part of ourselves that sees the everyday with Love and Hope, because of what It is.

If we are just this physical being, we will walk the road of life with heavy burdens and cast down eyes, with every meaningless step, enduring but not thriving. There is no joy in this journey, only the unending march to dissolution.

But, if instead, we are an eternal, ever expanding Conscious Energy, there is no path taken that is not an adventure, no chore done, not a service and no difficulty that cannot be turned into a blessing.

What do we connect with, that we might see Life with more grace? We welcome in our Greater Self. Help us understand our true Nature. Let us see beyond what can be seen but known with our Soul. "Hello?" We call out and are quietly answered. "Hello. I am here."

A Second Truth

Our Greater Self

It seems hard to understand, we can be something we are unaware of. But consider how consciousness can be focused to the exclusion of everything else.

When engrossed in a book or a movie, we lose sight of where we dwell and for that time, the entirety of our life. We become part of the story. But, when the last chapter is read, or the credits role and the lights turn on, suddenly we recall our Self.

Living in the world, is a play of sorts and when on stage, we are blind to what is in the wings. We become so entranced by our performance, we no longer recognize being an actor playing a role. It is not until we exit left, that we see behind the curtain and realize the theater we were in.

It's very easy to believe in what we see. This is how we experience perception as reality. It is extremely difficult though, to have faith in what is not seen ourselves.

If we tried to explain what the ocean was, to a man who lives in the desert, it would be almost impossible for him to understand. He'd consider us insane, as such an idea would violate his whole world view.

But, if we told him stories of sailing and described all the varieties of fish that live in its waters, slowly he becomes intrigued. Then, showing him pictures, he gets excited to see for himself. If he has the courage to take the journey and finally reaches the shoreline, he is forever transformed. He may go back home but will never be the same.

When he returns, some in his tribe will listen and others will laugh saying, he lost his mind among the sandy dunes. Though, he knows the truth and in his conviction, there is born the hope of something more.

We can have faith in what others tell us is true, but we must also experience it directly. It is not enough to sit and hear an adventurer's tale. We need to walk the road our self, to truly know what is at its end.

There is a Greater Self we are, that stands between the world and heaven, straddles time and eternity. This is the totality of our Being, the Wellspring from which we emerge to stand on the edge of an infinite ocean and feel the soft sands of the Earth between our toes.

We are the travelers, that sail in seas of Cosmic Energy, having come ashore to explore a new world. But the deeper we have ventured along its forest paths and mountain passes, the more dim our memory has gotten. Until at last, we know only the blazing sun and hot ground beneath our feet and forget the gentle waters from which we've come. Our true home is lost to the mists of myth and legend.

Throughout history, though, there are those who have been led into the wilderness and beyond, returning with Word of another Life we live. They stand as reminders of Reality and in their clarion Call, something within us stirs and humanity begins to awaken from its mortal dream.

Imagine standing on the prow of a boat, looking towards the horizon. We see the whitecaps crashing before us, the clouds in the sky moved by the wind, the sun setting in the west. But we don't see the vessel we're on, or the captain at the helm. We point a finger and head in that direction, never giving thought to who is steering the ship, that we go is all that matters.

Something is there we are not and yet we are. Who is here? I AM YOU, from a higher perspective.

Energy cannot be contained to any one form but can manifest itself in myriad expressions. As a Living Consciousness, we chose to embark on this human adventure. While part of our Mind dwells in the physical, the rest of Us remains non-physically focused. In each moment, we are in the world, but not of the world.

In crossing the threshold into material existence, however, we gradually lose full awareness of our Self. As we grow from a child into an adult, we let go of that knowledge, becoming immersed in society's belief system. We then, live our lives based on what we are taught, not what we are. Yet, our Truth still remains; held at deeper level of Being where our Source abides, though often, seemingly out of reach.

We can, if we choose, see human existence from a greater vantage point and from that height, have more clarity about the landscape below. In our journeys, we can know which roads to take and those to avoid; where the hidden pitfalls are, but also, the secret caves that hold real treasure.

We can, if we decide, discover ourselves in a new way and what before brought us pain, will now bring us peace and the hope we thought was gone, can be found again.

Envision what it would be like if we did not need money or physical things to live. How would we feel, waking up to having everything we need and doing anything we wanted? We felt no fear or guilt, only Love and saw the infinite possibilities of what can be achieved.

There would be a deep, sacred peace knowing our life was secured and our will fulfilled; a joy and excitement coming into the fullness of our potential; an unlimited sense to create whatever we desired. This is the happiness of heaven, the Reality of Inner Being.

In those moments of exaltation, when we look out on the world with love and compassion, we are remembering our True Nature and the Source from which we come. We look past the limits of the body and accept the unlimited power of nonphysical Energy. We regain that memory we cherished but forgot along the way.

I am Eternal.
I cannot die, cannot be hurt.
In all places I am a safe.
In all things I am blessed.
In all ways I am Loved.
I can be, do or have anything I desire.
My gift to myself is my gift to the Universe.
The meaning and purpose of my Life is found in my happiness.
I am here to bring my Light into the world
and share it with others.
I dwell always in the surety of my Existence.

This is the Reality of our Greater Self.

The Greater Reality

There is a greater Reality from which we come and where the Earth is planted and grows into existence; inconceivable to those who believe in time and space, it is infinite fields of Energy, that are limitless and unending, where All Conscious Beings have their existence. It cannot be seen with physical eyes, but its impact on our life is constant and profound.

Where do you think you go, when you die? In your dreams, are you in your bed, or in another dimension of your Greater Mind? Do thoughts appear out of nowhere or do they come from another realm and return after passing through?

As we were created, so we are. Though we appear in physical form, the essence of our Being is nonphysical. We are still Spirit and the body does not change that Truth. Our greater Life continues unabated.

**You are Spirit Now
and remain so forever.**

The Underneath

There is a place, underneath daily life, that stands as the foundation of the world, where all things are happening at once. There is no past, no future, only the Eternal Now.

Here is the Source of our Energy, the power that gives life to our decisions and actions. From it, we emerge into corporeal existence. It is where all events and circumstances have their origins before manifesting in form.

This Existence is invisible to the body's eyes, but can be known with inner vision. We must learn then, how to look with a different perspective.

Spirit cannot be seen with anything physical, but we can recognize Its Presence and so, understand it is there. When we regard each other as separate individuals with unrelated lives, we have a limited view. If for a moment, however, we can put aside our preconceptions and strive to think anew, another world can be seen.

What keeps us apart but the belief we are different. It is our judgments, that prevent us from appreciating the Oneness we share; our condemnations of each other as unworthy of love that keeps the body as our only reality.

But, when we look with Love, we begin to understand our Nature and see Spirit as our Truth. Then, a redeemed Earth appears in our Sight and we perceive the real world.

A Third Truth

We create the Life we live

Everything in our life, from the tiniest scratch to the most significant event, we create. Though few recognize the full extent of their influence on events.

There is nothing that comes upon us, we did not call to ourselves. Unseen, we are the ones behind the curtain directing the play. But, by not being fully aware of how things happen, we often don't take responsibility for what occurs and so, become victims of our own making.

The more we can accept our role, however, the greater control we gain. Then, in understanding the dynamics of manifestation, we can begin to deliberately choose our experience.

We form our Life by the decisions we make. Decisions are actions, but also thoughts we think and beliefs we hold. Outer conditions perfectly reflect our inner state. There are good events and bad, wanted and unwanted aspects, as there are positive beliefs and negative views, true perceptions and false illusions. All these find expression in the world.

What we live is a magnificent tapestry of everything within us, not one thing omitted. The external world allows us to know what we believe, because nonphysical ideas cannot be seen with the eyes, but can be known through their effects in physical reality. Thoughts turn to things and what things are present, reveals what stands behind them.

It is obvious, we form circumstances through our behaviors, actions and non-actions. What is not so apparent, is how conditions outside of our control arise and why they relate to our belief system.

We are Creators but do not create alone. All inner action is initiated by the Greater Self, in response to our state of mind.

As we feel, so we create.

Thoughts, which arise from beliefs generate feelings. Feelings are vibrations of energy within the mind, that extend outward. In that movement, there is an effect. When we think, the Universe responds.

Nonphysical Mind is a powerhouse that literally forms the world. All events have an energetic existence before manifesting in material terms.

This is the process of creating in the physical world:

We maintain a thought system.

We think thoughts that correspond to what we believe.

What we think creates feelings, which are vibrations of energy.

Vibrations of energy are held together in the nonphysical gathering strength. The more we focus on something the greater attention it is given. Energy added together becomes very powerful, until finally, it crosses the threshold into physical reality and appears in our circumstances.

Thoughts do not leave the mind unaffected. Every idea we have affects our state of being and determines how Energy is expressed. As a Consciousness, we cannot see our vibrational nature or that of others, nor know it through physical touch. But we can certainly feel it within.

We are Beings of Energy, translating thoughts into physical objects and experience. We take the inner content of our mind and give it form.

In a very real sense, the world is a workshop, where brave souls come to extend themselves into the clay of the Earth. It can be done in the spirit of Joy for the love of Creation, like a Sculptor forming a masterpiece. Or, in misery, toiling like a slave making bricks in the hot, summer sun. For most of us, there are moments of both.

So, what is the value or purpose of this?

It is a Cosmic Adventure, though too often feels like meaningless drudgery. But our Life is not meant to be endured, it is meant to be Lived. To Live deliberately though, we have to purposefully direct our Energy.

We are here to understand the power of our thoughts and how they create reality; to take responsibility for what we think and learn how to change our minds.

We come into the world full of hope and promise and try again to finish something started in the ancient past. It is another opportunity to take the final step in a journey begun long ago.

How can we create what we want?

To have anything we want, we have to decide what it is and focus only on that, to the exclusion of everything else and it will soon appear in our reality. It is that easy.

If we need more money, all we do is imagine what it feels like to be rich; envision what we'd buy or do and the happiness that brings. In that pure state of desire, we spend our days and within a short time, conditions arise supporting that view. Our thoughts of abundance quickly turn into material wealth. We ask and it is given without question.

This is the way Life works in truth and how a real Master forms their reality. It is the Law of Cause and Effect that rules the entire Universe.

What we give we receive.

For most, though we are creators, we are not Masters of our Self. We cannot so easily think a pure thought and hold it steady in awareness, until it appears in some form. Rather, we run the gamut from positive expectation to negative dread.

We have a strong idea of something we want and in that instant, we feel the exhilaration of getting it, luxuriating in its having. Universal Forces immediately respond to our desire and begin assembling all necessary components for its actualization. If we gave our undivided attention to its manifestation, it would soon appear in our day to day circumstances.

But we don't do that. Instead, we begin thinking contrary thoughts. Fear and worry creep in. We want it, but it's not practical. It's a fantasy, a pipe dream. In one moment, we have faith and in the next, doubt. Our being becomes filled with a mix of contradicting energies. We start along the road but stop and so, we never get anywhere. Then, we wonder why we always seem to be defeated in our aims. Is Fate against us?

Anyone who achieves a goal will say, they had an idea they believed in, knew it was possible, they could have it and deserved it. They may have met opposition from other people, but they did not oppose themselves and this made the difference.

The Law of Cause and Effect can be our best friend when single in determination and our worst enemy when lacking self-unity.

The Universe does not judge our wanting as right or wrong and decide who is blessed and who is cursed. It responds only to our expectations.

If we are in a desperate position and believe hope is impossible, then nothing can save us. We perpetuate negative circumstances by being miserable in them. We can spend long hours in church on our knees, praying night and day, but if we don't allow for miracles, we are doomed.

Good people won't get desires fulfilled while doing good deeds and still believing in their unworthiness. Evil people will succeed when wholly committed to twisted dreams, even though others are hurt or destroyed.

We do not exist in a void. Our Life is lived in an infinite field of Conscious Energy. As the material universe is structured around physical rules, so is nonphysical Reality bound by fundamental principles.

Universal Laws are impartial. There is not a person or a Force that chooses who gets what, based on human ideas of fairness and justice.

Life operates very simply:

What we focus on becomes our reality.
What we believe in becomes our Truth.

Focusing the mind is bringing to bear all the powers of creation. As we focus, we think, as we think we create.

In a very literal sense, our thoughts induce feelings, which are vibrations of our Energy. These vibrations have an attractive quality that draws to them elements of a similar vibrational nature. This process has been often called The Law of Attraction. It is Consciousness determining its own Realty, which is a foundational aspect of Inner Existence.

In this Universe, whose very essence is Love, we can have whatever we need, do whatever we want. Infinite Being does not question our Worthiness. When we ask, it is always given.

Yet, few live with this surety or rest in the deep peace knowing our Life is guaranteed. Rather, we stumble around in the darkness of uncertainty, trying to hold onto to what little we have and never daring to be bold in our Vision. We have immense resources within our grasp. Our Greater Self offers us everything. But, when that hand is extended, we turn away, sadly muttering, "too good to be true."

As human beings, we believe in what we see and the world as it appears in our sight, is a desperate battleground. Fantasies of wishes granted by waving a wand, are all that is offered here. Falling stars are signs, out there is a magical power that can be counted on. Neither though, offers true solace, because they are only imagined; dreamt in castles without rooms, that pretend something wonderful within, but in reality are mere facades. All the while, real hope stands by waiting our recognition, if we would just turn in its direction.

There is one question everyone asks and whose answer is the most sought-after treasure.

How can I get what I want?

We all seek for happiness and getting what we want makes us happy, because that is accomplishing our Will. In everything we do, we are looking to fulfill that purpose. There is no compromise. Only this brings peace. So, what stops us then?

Our life is the projected picture of inner conditions cast on the screen of the world. If we are unsatisfied, it is not events that are the source of dissatisfaction. It is our own unhappiness that creates those circumstances which makes us unhappy.

We often assume we build a life like a house, from the bottom up and outside in, then fill it with all we need for contentment. But Nature doesn't work this way. Everything that lives develops from the inside, extending itself outward as it grows.

When we are not living the Life we desire, we have to consider transforming thoughts and beliefs which are the foundation of our world. Then, when Cause is changed, effects must follow.

Here is the great Secret of the Universe. We always get exactly what we ask for. Though this does not appear so in the world, it is a fact of our Greater Reality.

There is nothing that comes to us against our will and all that we seek, we find. But who, looks at their life and sees the struggle and hardship we endure and believes this is true? Everyone wishes for things they never get and dreads some they do. The world though, is just the manifestation of inner thought. So, it is within ourselves we need to learn to discern between wanted and unwanted - what makes us happy and brings peace and what doesn't.

Ultimately, creating the reality we desire, is found in asserting our true Will.

We are powerless before what we don't want, but powerful in what we do.

A Fourth Truth

Purpose and Will

The key to happiness lies in the fulfillment of Will. We are only happy getting what we want. All misery, in whatever form, comes from discontentment.

Throughout the ages, enlightened masters have taught, the way to transcend suffering was to become free of desire and this is true. If we give up wanting anything, we can never feel the pain of not having it. Though, that does not guarantee a life of joy, simply one of detachment.

To withdraw from the day-to-day grind or choose to forego the emotional ups and downs of physical existence is a path some may travel. But, for those of us who are fully engaged in the human experience, the wheels of desire ever turn. We always crave something and when we don't get it, we suffer.

No one wants to be miserable or unsatisfied. It is common to think, if I had more money, this job or that lover I'd finally be at peace. That makes sense, since we have to make a living to pay bills and who doesn't want love and support. Because we have these wants, we assume fulfilling them is our one goal. And yet, the rich still suffer and for some, relationships are a battleground.

We cannot purchase a happy life with strips of paper or numbers on a screen. We can still feel alone in a crowded room and satisfaction will not come to a mind unsure of its direction. The real path lies in recognizing what we truly need and why we need it - in understanding our Will.

What is Will?

All that is exists because it was created and nothing undertaken is not motivated by a cause. Will is purpose, the intention behind all creation and the reason we do anything. It is the deciding factor in our decision making.

Desire is an aspect of existence, for what we want reflects what we are and what we are determines what we want.

We are two-part beings – matter and energy, physical and non-physical and each has its own interest. The body pursues one goal and the mind something else and neither can fulfill the other.

When we are hungry reading an inspirational book does nothing to fill our bellies. But having been fed, it can nourish our soul. Eating delicious ice cream when grieving, doesn't heal pain. But remembering a sweet moment with loved ones can bring us peace.

We are fulfilled according to our nature.

What is our Nature?

Our nature is what we are and how we live. Since we did not invent ourselves, we have to ask, "Who made me and why?"

The obvious answer is, we are born of our mother and father and why they had a child all depends. Were we conceived as an expression of their devotion and stand as a symbol of Love? Perhaps by accident instead, happy though it could have been, or not, but still a mistake. Then what would be our birthright? Or maybe it doesn't really matter how we came to be.

In reality, our parents did not conceive us. They simply passed on what was given them at their birth. We are more the inheritors of a process that began long ago, in the forgotten memories of an ancient past.

As a species, there is much that is unknown about our origins. Science can only speculate on how matter somehow gained self-motivation. Religions offer us stories and myths, though they lack physical evidence. But, what can be said with certainty is living cells began in two ways and depending on which we believe, determines our entire experience.

If physical life emerged in the shallow pools of primordial chaos by the accidental mixture of the right chemicals under the right circumstances, then it has no inherent purpose. It was not designed to be, but haphazardly caused by random lightning bolts charging the oceans of young planet. It just happened and so, it is forever without meaningful intent.

Yet, consider the outcome of such a thought system. Life would be some mysterious force that magically animates matter. Its beginnings unknown, its motivation not understood and because we lack knowledge of its source, we don't truly understand its nature.

In this view, what lives has no direction and serves no function. It is just a continuing cycle that could end without notice. Our only value is in passing on our DNA to the next generation to keep the race going, but for what reason we don't know. Our mind is just the by-product of the brain's activity with no independent existence and the soul is a myth.

When the body dies, you as a conscious being evaporate into nothingness and all that you are, all you have done and felt, your greatest dreams and desires, vanish into thin air and are no more.

Is there any meaning in that? What ends in death and disappears never to return, has a tenuous reality while it seems to be. Can this bring real joy, when all depression arises from meaninglessness.

Instead, what if all physical matter is a manifestation of an unending Conscious Energy and every atom and molecule has a non-physical counterpart from which it emerges. What if the entire Universe, from the big bang through the evolutions that shaped life on Earth was willfully guided by a broader intelligence?

If this is true, then the world and everything in it, was Caused to be, not by happenstance, but by will.

If we believe we are only a body, destined to have a temporary existence, what small happiness we find will be limited to the body's continuation and everything we encounter that opposes its survival we will fear and dread.

But, if we are something more than just a physical organism that walks aimlessly about in search of food and a warm place to sleep, there is the hope of discovering this greater purpose and the true nature of being human.

How can we know the Truth?

If we don't know something's origin, we can still understand its cause by what it does and its nature by what it wills.

A thing born of chaos has no order to its behavior. There is no pattern or rhythm to its actions. It doesn't have a direction because it is not motivated by intent. But, what is made to serve a function follows certain principles that reveal its creation and ultimately its Creator.

What do we do and seek for in Life?

The fundamental goal of all life is to live and so, everything we pursue relates to our will to continue living.

As physical beings, we require food, water and shelter to keep the body alive and because we think it is the source of our identity, it becomes our goal to meet those demands.

It is the reason we work to make money, go shopping for groceries and clothes, buy homes and cars; all help us in achieving that aim. If we did not identify with the physical form, we might not care if it withered away.

It would seem then, we should always be content with dinner on the table, clothes on our back and a roof over our head, because only that is required to survive. But for most, that is not enough.

There is part of each of us that is unsatisfied with subsisting. Eventually, we ask ourselves, "Is this all there is?" Even those who achieve fame and fortune, wonder the same.

We know we are driven to sustain our presence on this Earth. But we also recognize, at a deeper level, something is missing in a life solely dedicated to fulfilling the flesh. It is a shallow existence, whose roots are easily upended with any passing storm and though denied, we dimly acknowledge without substance, such trappings provide little comfort when needed most.

Invariably, those who search for understanding come to a place of great uncertainty the dark night when we question, what is the point of sustaining the body if it dies? Is there any value in all that effort and struggle, if it amounts to nothing and comes to an end leaving no trace behind, like a cloud that takes shape and for a brief moment seems to have reality, only to quickly dissipate back into thin air?

Perhaps the answer lies in a more profound yearning. We want our lives to mean something. This alone shows, there is another aspect to our being that calls to us, seeking to be heard.

What is the meaning of Life?

The meaning of anything, lies in the purpose it serves. When we ask what is the meaning of our life, we are really asking what is my reason for being? Why am I on this Earth? What, if anything, am I here to do?

The only real function of the body is to join with other bodies to copulate and continue the species. Other than that, we do not aide in the evolution of the natural world.

From a nihilistic point of view, human beings take more than they give. Building cities, plowing fields, paving roads, do nothing to keep the world spinning. We pollute the air, the rivers and the oceans. We kill other creatures for food and sport. We don't live in harmony with nature but exploit all its resources for our own selfish gain.

Humankind, does not benefit the planet, when considered an accidental happening, whose entire existence here is but a blight on its fertile fields; a blaring siren in its quiet forests. What duty would we owe the Earth, if we are all the motherless progeny of an unknown father? Where is our connection to the land?

And yet, we wake up every morning with some hope of a worthwhile day. No one runs eagerly to a boring job doing meaningless work. Who skips down the sidewalk of a nameless street, on their way to an anonymous life filled with drudgery? We do not exist just to eat, sleep and procreate.

We all desire more; to feel valued, to know our struggles and sacrifices are not for nothing. We want to imagine great dreams are possible because we live in a Universe that actually cares about us and our happiness, that our life matters. We create music and art, write books and stories, develop sciences and philosophies, play games and sports, which are not necessary for survival but somehow, essential for living.

The spirit of the human race has an unrelenting passion for self-expression that transcends the temporal and shouts to those who would listen:

"You are not born by accident. You have a Source. You are the extension of unfathomable Energy that makes Itself manifest in matter, a world of flesh and bone. You and the Earth are One and bound to each other. It honors you, as you must honor It.

You came here for a reason. Look for it within and discover the true purpose of your life. Find peace and happiness in this brilliant understanding, for all the Universe is but waiting your welcome."

How do we find our Purpose?

It seems strange we are unaware of the answer to this simplest of questions. It is inherent in our nature and if we lack understanding, we don't know what we are. Yet is this possible, to be a thing we know not?

Yet, it must be, because how many can say they are completely certain of their reason for being? Unless they think they have none and make their own.

Without question, we are physical creatures and many consider the body as the foundation of their Self. But what is not fully understood is, we are also non-physical energy and our identity is really an aspect of inner beingness.

This is the way perception works. What we focus on becomes our reality and nothing else can enter our field of awareness. We only see what we believe is real and even the mind can think the body is more tangible than itself.

That we are compelled to constantly give our attention to the physical world, is enough for us to lose sight of our greater existence as an Eternal Consciousness. But we can, if we choose, learn to see beyond the mortal to the everlasting and come into a broader comprehension of the nature of personal reality.

All that we are is always present; though too often unrecognized, it can be known. To unravel the mystery of ourselves, we need to become more aware of our inner reality and what is dim grows brighter, what is obscure becomes obvious.

While in the world, we have a dual nature and both matter and energy, have different goals. Sometimes they seem to compete and we endure the stress of that struggle. Other times they are aligned and enjoy the ease of that flow. Ultimately they both seek the same outcome – achieving our purpose.

Our first purpose is to survive.
Our greater purpose is to live.

Our first purpose is the most immediate. It centers around our need to maintain the body's existence. In our society, we are ruled by the laws of economics. We must pay for everything. Some can grow their own food and build their own house, but even they need to buy land and supplies.

We have to do what it takes to make money. You can be the greatest painter alive, but if no ones buys your paintings, how can you live? If you are at a party and some leave for work, but you can stay because you have no job, of what value is that freedom, if you are homeless after it ends? Most criminal activity is not for pleasure, but for profit and even spiritual leaders make a salary.

Our entire lives, we are taught to be realistic. Chasing after dreams or fantasies are only encouraged if there is some hope of gain. Above all else, our priority is ensuring whatever we pursue yields financial reward.

So, everything we do, the decisions we make, what paths we follow and the roads we travel all lead to supporting our physical existence. For many, this seems the wisest course of action and as promised, should lead to a happy, fulfilled life. Though unknowingly, it does not.

Most people never go beyond their first purpose. They become so preoccupied with the world, they rarely give thought to anything else. When they find some small contentment, there is still an uneasy feeling though, a gnawing sense of incompleteness they are afraid to face. In the back of their minds, the deeper questions about life and death have not been answered, but linger, as silent warriors against their peace.

There is more to our Being than what appears in form. There is the Content of our Greater Self, that is the source of our true meaning.

We are not born to just live a physical life. The body is not the driver, but the driven. It is only the vessel that holds the spirit and has no motivation of its own.

Intention is an aspect of Energy, being part of its nature. Energy is never static, but always in motion. It is action not stasis. In truth, we can never understand our reason for being looking to the body. It does not know. It is not Cause but effect.

**It is only in the Mind
where our true purpose is found.**

Our greater purpose is not about heroic deeds, or saving the world, being born with a mission, or achieving specific goals. It is more fundamental and inclusive. It arises from what the mind is and is faithful to its Source.

The mind does not grasp for air like the body, or suffer hunger pains. It is never cold or shivers under ragged blankets on a winter's night. It stumbles not and breaks a limb, nor does it age and grow old. The mind is eternal. Its motivation is not to survive because it cannot die and yet, it still seeks to Live.

What is the Life of Mind?

The life of the mind is founded in what it does - conceiving thoughts as patterns of energy and experiencing the flow of that energy as emotion. So its life is in its thinking and feeling. But also and more fundamentally, it creates self or identity.

What we are is a concept - an abstract idea that has no dimension or limitation but has meaning and reality. This image of ourselves we hold in our minds and how we give it life, is by extending it outward.

The whole function of the world, is to allow us to express this nonphysical content into physical form – to turn our thoughts into things.

It doesn't matter if we are a homeless drug addict living in the streets, scrounging for a meal and our next fix, or the head of vast empire sitting on a gilded throne, adored by their royal court. Both are equally and as powerfully, manifesting the idea of themselves in material existence.

We sustain the body because we use it to communicate what is within. But beyond this need, there is the primary motivation for self-extension.

Our will is the extension of our self.

How do we extend ourselves?

Creating anything in this world begins with a decision. Choices are not just about doing, they are also about believing. What we think we are, we manifest in daily life and once having decided, we must share it with others to make it a reality.

We achieve nothing sitting around daydreaming, if we also don't get off the couch and do what is required to bring it about. If we don't speak, we are not heard and there is no response. So we are left with just an idea of something, but not its physical appearance.

We can walk around telling everyone we are a great writer, but if no one reads our work and agrees, how valid is that belief? We could be the heir of a kingdom seeking their throne, but if we go unrecognized would we be seated?

Our will can only be accomplished through sharing.

Sharing is giving but also being received. If we give and it is not accepted, then it is not shared.

Our will cannot be fully accomplished, unless it is acknowledged by someone other than ourself. Regimes throughout history have fallen, simply because people stopped listening to their leaders, as many slaves found freedom in rebelling against a master's dictates.

Certainly, we can do things alone with no help or approval. But it is limited and eventually we encounter people on the road, who will either let us pass or stand in our way.

If I am hungry and go to the store to buy food, but they won't sell me any because I have no money, I cannot eat. I can try to impose my will on them by force or even deception. But, I might get caught and put in jail and that doesn't serve me.

In the same manner, if we are in a foreign country and have money but the shopkeeper doesn't speak our language, we still cannot get what we want and go unsatisfied.

Our Will is to be Known,
to be Understood and to be Accepted.

The act of creation is threefold. It begins with an idea of wanting or being, seeking manifestation. It is then expressed through words and actions that can be understood. When opposed, it remains a mental abstraction, but if accepted, it becomes a material actuality.

Oftentimes though, what we want we don't get. We state our desires, but the world doesn't answer. The circle is never completed and it is in being rejected that we suffer.

All unhappiness is the denial of will.

I want to be a rich and famous performer. But my acting or singing is not considered very good. I feel I am talented, but no one casts me in a role or books me for a gig. My fantasies of stardom are relegated to a tiny bedroom with my adoring audience just a reflection in the mirror. I get depressed and feel life is meaningless.

The more I invest in making it big, the greater my disappointment will be if I don't succeed and sadly, the failed aspirations of today become the deep regrets of tomorrow.

For many of us, though we may sit at the table of a bountiful feast, Life can seem an unending struggle to get fed. We see everyone as out for themselves and are only included, when fitting into someone else's agenda.

We never get the promotion we want or advance at the company we work; passed over for those less deserving but more ingratiated with the boss. Our opportunity to make more money is limited by who we know, or the color of our skin - a thousand other reasons we are not considered good enough.

We can't find the right person to love and care for us, as we would them, if only given a chance; not judged by our appearance but our heart.

People around us get ahead, while we feel constantly left behind, scrambling for what meager scraps may come our way. So we shake our fist at the Universe and shout, "Where is the justice? When do I get my break?"

It is a bleak situation indeed, looking to others for support, if they are only out for themselves. What is our hope, having to depend on self-serving individuals that don't care what we want? Should we give up then, wanting more?

How can we achieve our will?

There are many ways we try to convince people to give us what we want, especially when we feel they are against us.

We can be cajoling, hoping our pleas might strike a chord and they respond with some compassion. Those who want to be less vulnerable, play the game of deception, convincing a mark to give them what they seek in exchange for a great deal. Usually, relying on another's greed or taking advantage of a difficult situation.

If we have a certain passion, we may present our views to the crowd and rally the troops to achieve a common goal. Lastly, when all else fails, we resort to threats.

Throughout history, we have glorified villains who use physical aggression to impose their will on others. In many countries, they have been crowned kings and queens, while every dictator has ruled through fear and oppression.

Bank robbers are notable characters in movies, who steal whatever they desire, in complete disregard of the law. Society celebrates gangsters who use force to achieve submission, because they just take what they want. Though, we ourselves might not be so brutal, secretly we admire their ferocity.

Who has not been tempted to imagine resorting to coercion, when in a desperate situation? Or wished they had a scary friend to intimidate an adversary?

Ultimately, whatever approach we choose, it comes down to one thing – it's all about Power.

The key to happiness
lies in the power to fulfill our will.

Its almost useless to want something without being able to bring it to fruition, it only becomes a misery instead of a joy. Most ordinary people, however, see themselves as not having much influence over their circumstances. So how then can we really live a happy life?

Our great failure, is misunderstanding true power. In our world, we mistakenly believe it is about controlling reality, or other people. But having power is a creative attribute, not a possession. It is inherent in what we are, not what we have.

Power is the ability to affect change.

It is our natural inclination, when dissatisfied, to want things to be different. Anything that lives is driven to self-fulfillment. The challenge we all face, in one way or another, is creating the reality we desire.

When we depend on ourselves alone, we are limited by our individual experience and capabilities. We can accomplish nothing, if we don't know how and more so, if we lack the necessary resources.

For us, knowledge and money are power. So, if either is missing, then obtaining our goals is challenging. Many people know what they want; most people cannot achieve it and while this is true in the world, thankfully, it is not the Greater Truth.

No one is ever powerless.

If power is an attribute of what we are, it is apparent why we feel powerless believing we are a body.

As human beings, we have long wished for the ability to master our environment and events. Our society is enthralled with the idea of moving objects with our minds, shooting energy from our hands and lasers from our eyes. It is a prevalent theme in movies and television.

Perhaps an alien artifact crashes to the Earth and in touching it, we are infused with an otherworldly energy. We inject a serum or take a pill and somehow, mysteriously we are transformed into a super hero.

Such fantasies are imagined, because at a subconscious level, we recognize physical beings never have, nor ever will possess such attributes. Bodies are inherently weak and vulnerable. They are bound to the Earth and cannot survive on their own. A wrong twist of the neck or small wound can end its life and no story, no matter how thrilling, will change that. Is it no wonder then, we yearn to be invincible and secretly lament our frailty?

Though, why do we cling to such illusions, when real promise can be found? There is no possibility the body can be anything else. But, we are more than flesh and bone. We are non-physical energy and that is where our true power lies.

What is our True Power?

The mind is energy and the seat of Being. It is from this power-house, physical reality emerges into existence.

So yes, we can alter matter, command the forces of nature and move mountains. We can heal the sick, raise the dead and walk on water. Though, it is not with ego-based thinking, focused on the world that we can achieve such miraculous feats. It is only the Mind of the Greater Self, who dwells in timelessness, that can so dominate the world.

But in how many is this Self fully known and understood? It is the rare Soul who can live a human life and remember they are Eternal Consciousness. Those we call Visionaries, Saints, Prophets, Krishna, Buddha and Christ.

For the rest of us, though we have the potential, we are not yet capable. Still, our forgetfulness does not change our inherent nature and we can, if we choose, slowly regain that awareness.

Unknowingly, every moment of every day, we are forming our life experience using the power given us in our Creation. Would it be, that we have been imbued with a Will and no way to fulfill it?

**The power to create our reality
comes from within.**

To harness Creative Power and use it deliberately, we must come into a deeper understanding of our relationship with Inner Being; discover the meaning and purpose of our life; know the difference between Truth and Illusion and finally, walk the path that leads to the fulfilment of our Will.

When that is accomplished, the whole Universe is ours to command.

A Fifth Truth

Truth and Illusion

What is Truth?

The Truth of anything comes from its creation. The creator of something decides what it is. In this sense, we form our personal truth about the world and ourselves through our perceptions.

At this level, though, what is true for me is not true for you, because we may not share the same belief system. One person's dream could be another's nightmare. We can agree on the facts of a circumstance or event. But still, facts lack meaning and are open to interpretation.

For something to be true, it must always be the same under all circumstances, at all times and apply to everyone. As it was in the past, so it is in the present and must be in the future. Its hallmark is constancy. Beliefs then, though they can reflect reality, are not Truth since they are variable and subject to change.

To know what something is, we must ask its Cause. But, nowhere on the Earth, is there a mountain we can climb and its peak find the Source of All There Is and pose this simplest question. "What is the meaning of life?"

There is no place we can travel to with our tiny spaceships and discover the reason behind the existence of the stars. Or, peer into the night sky with our telescopes and find an explanation.

Here is our greatest obstacle to understanding. No one by themselves knows. When we ask the most basic questions about who we are, they go unanswered, because we did not create ourselves.

If there is a Creator of the Universe, how many truly speak to Him or Her, or Them?

Some preachers say they talk to God, but invariably, such revelations are proven false. So again, we are disappointed or, for some, proven right there is no such being. Others are satisfied with reading ancient spiritual texts and live their lives them.

Those who prefer to believe everything is born of chaos, will see any seeking for purpose as a fruitless search, because there is none. Most of us, however, simply push aside or ignore the deeper issues, seeing no hope for resolution.

We all want to be happy. Yet, if we don't know what we are, how can we ever make choices and decisions that fulfill our will?

The bleak despair of depression and hopelessness we often suffer through, is rooted in this basic of all human dilemmas – not knowing where to find the Answer.

Throughout history, there are those who have achieved the state of enlightenment and reached nirvana; prophets who spoke with angels from above and even the proclaimed son of God himself, who was born on Earth to bring the good news of eternal Life.

If we follow them, we may find solace in the frameworks their teachings provide. Faith though, without personal experience, becomes a myth; a story told long ago that may or may not be real.

In our daily lives, we all find some measure of joy and though unrecognized, we do come into a greater recognition. But, it is not enough to occasionally stumble upon insight along the way. There must be a more deliberate path we can take that leads to Reality, even if we never see visions or encounter Divine Beings.

When we are willing to put aside our need for immediate proof, there is an unexpected road that opens we can travel and finally discover who and what we are.

We are not absolutely certain about what we see. Using perception, we must infer meaning, being based on belief, not knowledge. The truth of a thing comes only from its Source, or by having a direct experience of what is created. While we are not the Originator, we are the life that is lived and so, we can understand our nature and eventually our Cause, by knowing ourselves.

The doorway to Truth
is through self-awareness.

You are fully self-realized when you know all aspects of your being – how you function and why, your reason and purpose. But how many can claim such depth of understanding? In fact, human existence is characterized by a profound lack of awareness. We see, hear and touch, but we don't Know.

Though we have a body, it operates out of our field of recognition and what we do understand has not been learned directly, but, from studying other bodies.

No one can say how they turn food into energy, how they heal a wound or keep their heart beating. We can watch our breathing, but are unable to change it. We feed the body, nourish it and care for it, though we cannot make it grow. We have a limited role in its continuation and are unable to control its functioning.

Material existence then, will never be where Truth is found, because it cannot be illuminated. Our only hope is in what can and that is Consciousness.

Self-understanding can only be found
In the mind, where the self exists.

There are two aspects to knowing one's self. First is understanding the mind and its contents. Second, is recognizing, if what we think and believe reflects our true nature.

The Mind is not the brain. It is a structure of non-physical energy, that is always active and never sleeps. It exists beyond time and space, does not age or grow old. It is ever present, both powerful and unlimited. Rarely do we comprehend its full ability.

It is profoundly creative, whose function is to harness energy, transforming it into fields of actuality. It is the hub of creation where all states of Being are known and understood. Aside from the body, It is where our Self experience's Life.

In the mind, energy is channeled along the lines of our thinking. As thoughts expand outward we experience them as feelings, which leads to decisions that form our physical circumstances. We then perceive those conditions as supporting evidence of our world view and this is how personal reality is created.

Most of us, however, are blind to this process and assume what we perceive is actually happening. But outer events are never as they appear to be. Rather, they stand as symbols for deeper inner states.

Because we cannot see beliefs, a method for recognizing them is necessary. The whole reason for manifesting non-physicality into matter, is to provide a learning environment where what is hidden can be seen.

Ultimately, all Life is driven to live by its nature. It is a fundamental Law of the Universe, a thing can only beget as it was begotten, only exist as it was conceived.

We were created free and can think as we choose. But, when we cling to falsity, we are compelled to undo it.

Every event, encounter, condition, situation, regardless if we consider it good or bad, a blessing, a disaster, wanted or undesired, is no more and no less than, another opportunity to decide, if what we think, is what we truly are.

In this regard, we consider the Earth a school room, though the lessons here are not educational, since all Knowledge is contained within. Instead, we learn if we are living in accord with our creation.

Real success or failure is not as the world defines it, of attaining fame and fortune, position and power. It is lost or found in the realization of the true reason for the human experience.

Our purpose in Life is to live in Truth.

The determination is simply this: Are we happy and at peace, filled with Love, an abiding sense of well-being and abundance; have no fear, guilt or trepidation of any kind?

If we answer yes, then we truly Understand our Self and stand in alignment with our Source. If the answer is no, however, then we think thoughts and hold beliefs that are not reflective of Greater Reality.

When we are joyful, it is because we are fulfilling our will. When we are in conflict or unhappy in some way, it is going unfulfilled. Yet, it is our perceptions that establish how we feel.

Circumstances are just conditions and have no inherent meaning. It is what we ascribe to events that decides our experience and the center of all decisions is the idea of who we are.

Our primary motivation is to live in reality, for it is only there we find the surety of our existence. So, necessarily, we must think our beliefs are true, never considering they could be false.

Since Truth is immutable and cannot be changed, in our unhappiness, is it not better that we are wrong instead of being right?

We are never separated from Inner Being, even though we may be completely unaware of Its existence. Our life, however, is dependent on this unseen Self and without knowing why, we feel the negative effects of thinking we are alone.

Seeing through the body's eyes, feeling its movements, pains and pleasures does not alter the non-physical. We are bound by the same Universal Laws, regardless of where we imagine ourselves to be and this is the real basis of our life.

The world does not rest on its own foundation, but stands on the bedrock of a more expansive Reality where Existence is Eternal and Unending. It is from here we emerge in the corporeal, like a tree whose roots are buried deep In the Earth and rises up to spread its branches out across the landscape.

When we are not at peace, at any level, from the smallest discomfort to the greatest despair, we are not living in harmony with Truth. It then becomes our purpose to uncover those errors in thinking and have them corrected.

Our Belief System

Our belief system is the main source of our thinking while in physical form. From it, we see a whole world of our own making. Each one of us has a unique view with a different experience and at a certain level it is valid. But as we go deeper, we discover, what we considered indisputable fact is actually subjective opinion.

It is precisely the idea we perceive correctly – we see it as it is - that keeps us bound to negative life experience. So, we must come to accept that our perceptions are relative to our thought system and not absolute.

An important step in self-awareness, is found in recognizing our beliefs, for it is with them we form our reality. But, they are not obvious, nor easily seen. More often they lie hidden behind layers of ideas we assume are true. We do not question their validity and so, they remain behind the scenes directing the action, yet never on stage in full view.

But, if we are ever to understand ourselves, it is crucial we bring them out into the open and have them judged as reflecting what is true or what is false.

Perception is not seeing with our eyes, but with our mind. When we interact with the world, we must interpret what something is and give it a meaning because we don't Know anything with certainty. We do this using our substitute for knowledge and that is belief.

In looking outward, we are not directly aware of what is within. Thoughts come to us, as a quick moving stream that is virtually automatic. In the moment, we don't actively realize what we are thinking, even though we immediately feel their result.

But, we can learn of cause by its effects and recognize what we believe by understanding our experience.

Feelings are the indicator of beliefs.

To uncover a belief then, which is the idea of what something is, we start at the end and work towards the beginning by asking ourselves this basic question, "How does this make me feel?"

This situation makes me feel upset.

This circumstance makes me feel threatened

This person's actions make me angry.

This event makes me happy.
This nonaction brings me peace.

As the first step is recognizing our emotional state, a second step is clarifying it further.

I am upset because I think this is something negative.
I am afraid because I think this is something threatening.
I am angry because I think this is an injustice.
I am happy because I think this is something I want.
I am at peace because I think this fulfills my will.

At this point, we make a transition in understanding, from thought to belief.

I am upset because *I believe* this is something negative.
I am afraid because *I believe* this is something threatening.
I am angry because *I believe* this is an injustice.
I am happy because *I believe* this is something I want.
I am at peace because *I believe* this fulfills my will.

In the realm of mind, belief is just something we have thought over and over and accepted as valid. Ideas come and go and seem transient in their nature. But, as we go deeper they become more constant and are held steadily by Truth. It then becomes the basis in which we see the world.

It is here, we can begin to peel back the outer layers, to reach the center by being more specific.

I am upset when I have no money, because I believe without it I cannot pay my bills.

I am afraid being in a high place, because I believe I can fall and get injured.

I am angry when I see someone being mistreated, because I believe people deserve justice.

I am happy when I meet someone I connect with, because I believe we can form a relationship.

I am at peace when I am at sitting on my deck alone, because I believe I am not being disturbed.

The more we look at our ideas, they expand. Our experience of anything is never about a single belief, but is more of a composite, as a tree limb has many branches, with clusters of leaves.

If I have no money and can't pay my bills, they will repossess my car and turn off my electricity. I will be unable to buy food and they will foreclose on my house.

If I am up too high, a strong wind could come and blow me off the edge I will fall down to the ground. Or, if I am standing too close to the window and it breaks and I fall out.

I get so mad when I see people being mistreated or oppressed. It's not right. It's wrong.

I am so happy being in a relationship with someone special, who cares about me and I care about them.

It so calm here, The weather is nice and no one is around. There is nothing negative going on.

Eventually, in our journey within, we come to core beliefs. They are usually broad and generalized.

In this world, money is the power to live, without it you cannot survive.

Getting injured threatens my well-being.

I would be happy if I could change everything that makes me unhappy about the world.

To be alone is a miserable existence.

I am at peace when no one is attacking me.

Our beliefs about the world are endless. It is impossible to look at all of them. But, no matter how varied and seemingly unrelated, they all come to down to a single idea.

The foundation of any thought system is always the idea of our self. From this center we judge our circumstances and determine how we experience them.

When we lack money we feel afraid because we cant pay our bills. If we cant pay our bills we can lose everything we have acquired.

This is a fact of our world and so we assume how we feel about it is true and cannot be changed. And yet, really what we are experiencing is the idea of ourself without money.

If I had no money today but knew I could get more anytime, would I still be terrified of having no money?

The real reason we are afraid, is because we believe we lack the ability to get money when we need it. Since money in our society represents power, then this is a fundamental belief in being powerless.

If I fell off a roof, in all likelihood I would get injured, unless I could fly and then would I be concerned with falling? Really, this fear of getting injured is because I believe I am inherently vulnerable.

Being unhappy about how others are treated, is the idea inner experience is determined by the world and cannot be controlled by us, because our will is weak without any influence.

If we take any feeling and follow it back, it always leads to some fundamental idea about Who and What we are.

This evaluation is a necessary step to happiness and peace. But, it is not enough to only recognize what we believe about ourselves. Once we reach this point, the real question becomes:

How do we know if a belief is true or false?

The fundamental problem we all face is that we believe our thoughts are valid, otherwise we would not think them and because the mind is energy and all ideas have the same power and effect.

The strength of our belief in something, is not the basis for evaluating whether it is true. We often have faith in falsehood with greater conviction then truth itself. But, we can learn to distinguish between the two.

In this world, we experience the physical through sensation and the nonphysical through concepts. We know what it is functioning properly by ease and when dysfunctional, by pain. In the same manner, when we are thinking truly we feel at peace and when thinking falsely, we feel conflict.

In the body, discomfort is the sign something is wrong. In the mind, it is the sign something is false.

We can determine if a thought is true or false by how it makes us feel. If it goes against our True Nature, we feel the discord.

All belief is self-belief and so, what we think about anything is really a reflection of a deeper idea about ourselves. Consequently, we judge all things based on our Will. So, what is right or true, is in alignment with it and brings happiness. What is wrong or false, is out of alignment and creates some form of distress.

Will is the motivating force behind life. It is why we do anything. It arises from what we are. We are a Living Energy that seeks continuation and expansion. So everything we do reflects that fundamental desire.

Unlike with the eyes, which do not create what they see, seeing with the mind is not a passive process. Perception is deciding what we want, by giving something a meaning and so, it is an active decision. We see what we want to see.

But the question still remains and needs to be answered - Are we perceiving truly?

If we created ourselves, then our perceptions would always be correct, since we decide what to believe. But, we did not create ourselves and the journey to understanding is not about what we want to be, but What We ARE.

We arise from a Deeper Self, so we must always look within for Truth. No one speaks to their Inner Being as one person to another. Neither are we in communication with this greater Self in any obvious manner. But, we are part of Its existence, otherwise we would not exist.

Inner Being maintains the body and is the source of our consciousness. Our awareness, however, is limited to the personality we know, because our attention is on physical experience. So, we become oblivious to other realities. Yet, they are not totally unknown to us and can be recognized.

Our will comes from our deeper self as an expression of our Being. We know what we are by what we want. Further, we realize if we are getting what we want, by how we feel.

The fulfillment of Will that leads to happiness, can only come from being true to our Nature. Emotions then, are the guide to understanding if perceptions are true or false.

We are accustomed to believing the world is separate and outside us, that what we think has no bearing on reality and our feelings are irrelevant. But our whole life experience is not based on what the world is, but what we think it is and subsequently, what we think about ourselves.

We can choose how we see the world, but cannot choose the result of that choice. We cannot decide a situation is negative and feel at peace, cannot attack another and feel Love, cannot see suffering and be happy.

Why is that? Why are we not overjoyed when in a desperate situation, or tremble when feeling threatened? Why do we feel good when helping someone and worthy when being loving?

The reason is the Mind, what it is and the purpose it serves. Mind's function is to extend Energy and when expressed truly, it creates reality. But, mind can also make unreality through the projection of falsity.

When the Mind extends what is True, we feel the rightness of that as Peace, Joy, Love and Happiness.

When we project what is false, we feel the wrongness of that as fear, guilt, anger, sorrow, despair and suffering.

Though we cannot change what reality is, having been created in freedom, we can choose to extend Truth or project un-Truth and we learn what we are doing by our state of mind.

Illusion is unreality. But, because the mind is energy and where belief is held, both true and false ideas have effects.

Illusions are false ideas we believe are true
and experience as real.

Illusion is not nebulous, like a mist that quickly vanishes with the wave of a hand. We experience it fully, believing in it, though it is based on falsehood.

The Truth of Existence comes from the Creator of All That Is. Whether we have faith there is such a Great Being or not, does not change the fact, we are not our own invention. We did not give ourselves life, neither did our parents, nor does the Earth. We are something more than what we perceive, something vaster then we know.

We hear the whispers in our minds, of a ancient song we once sang and would sing again, if we but knew our Greater Reality.

The world is a place of forgetting and also a place of remembering. It is here we get lost in the illusions of separate bodies, of time and space, lack and limitation. But, it is also here, we can begin a journey that meanders through the landscapes of the world, slowly winding its way within. Into the secret caverns kept hidden we enter and find the great treasure of Life, that is our Self.

The True Self vs the False Self

In our minds, we all hold the idea of who and what we are and every thought and feeling that arises, is in response to this self-concept. But, an image is not the thing it represents. It shifts and moves and is altered by circumstances. So, it cannot be that which is changeless

What are we then, that is always constant, always the same under all conditions?

We are Mind Energy, that is the essence of our true nature. This mind is pure consciousness or spirit, at one with all that exists. It is eternal and unlimited. But, when the mind sees itself as a body, symbolically speaking, it splits in two. The part that knows it is eternal energy and the part that believes it is matter and we, as the conscious self, stand in the middle.

The mind that thinks it is a physical being, we call the ego. Ego is the idea we are separate and apart from all livings things, whose life begins at its beginning, ends at its ending and while it lives is self-sustaining. This is the false self, because the foundation of its thought system is not based on Truth. Our true self, reflects the deeper reality of Inner Being.

While we are in the world, we experience both aspects of our Mind and are constantly deciding which part is real, which is not and what we choose, determines our entire experience.

It is impossible to deny the body, but equally impossible to deny the mind. Yet, we cannot be two opposing things at once. One must be a misidentification and this is the fundamental problem we all encounter, in one form or another.

The journey then, to self-understanding, is learning how to distinguish between the Self of Truth and the self of illusion.

For the mind who knows not what it is, enlightenment comes along the road to peace. When we don't understand who we are, what to do or where to go, the guide we follow is the Light of Joy.

Yet, most people imagine such simplicity is naive. We are conditioned to believe life must be difficult, happiness is impractical and there is some inherent flaw in human beings, that makes them undeserving of goodness.

It doesn't make sense to a hardened world, that our Greater Reality is far easier, and gentler then society's accepted rules of pain and struggle. But, it is so.

Complexity is of the ego, wanting to obscure what is very simple. We are happy when acknowledging Inner Being and disturbed, to any degree, listening to our mortality. Yet, which is valid?

True Ideas bring happiness.
False ideas bring misery.

If I have an overdue bill and thinking about it makes me feel badly, it is not being late in paying that is awful, but the idea I don't have the resources needed and am incapable of getting them. It is the belief I am without any real power. But more so, it is the reason for being powerless.

In our society, we don't just think and money appears. We have to do something to get it and what does the doing of anything? Is it not the body?

If I am afraid of falling and getting hurt because I am vulnerable, what gets hurt? What has little influence and can be separated out from others and be alone? Is it not the body?

Though, we may not recognize it, when we see ourselves as unlimited Energy instead, what is our experience?

I am at peace when I feel strong.

I am joyful when I feel free.

I have a sense of worth when I have a purpose.

I am filled with love, when my life is supported and I support the life of others.

Every situation, condition or event is always asking us the question, What am I? and how we feel is our answer. If we encounter circumstances with a positive outlook, confidence and surety, then we are coming from the recognition of our inherent power and strength as Eternal Energy. If we are negative and complain, feel anxious, are worried, have a sense of dread and foreboding, then we are coming from the fear of being a helpless, weak, vulnerable body.

The Search for Truth

Most people live their lives unaware of their greater reality. There is little impulse for something else. What then sets them on the road to greater understanding?

Our will is constant and we are always looking for its fulfillment. We only start searching when missing what we treasure, or lost what we value and what is valued most, but our Life.

We begin seeking more when what we have is less. We start asking questions when the answers we have are unsatisfying. We want to learn, because what we think is lacking. When we are not at peace, filled with joy, feel threatened or afraid, we will look for change because our will is going unfulfilled.

It seems a great paradox, we can be what we are completely unaware of and not see what is there in reality, yet see instead what is in illusion. But that is the essence of the physical experience.

Being human means we are born on this Earth, without memory of having existed before. The person we seem to be, began at birth and developed along the way, formed in childhood and now lived as an adult. What we learn about ourselves, is what the world teaches us. It is a lesson though, that does not always bring joy.

But ever with us, there is the hint of something else in the background. Perhaps, far off in the distance quietly watching; above the drama on the stage, intently listening and offering another view; a new way of seeing things that brings peace instead of pain.

Are you willing to hear a different Voice that speaks of happiness, of the guiltless self, unlimited in its potential with the power and freedom to be anything it desires? For such is what the Truth proclaims.

Yet, if what we are is always there, why do we have such a miserable picture of ourselves? Is it that we don't listen? Or do we hear instead, what marches to a mournful drumbeat, on its slow and merciless walk to its inevitable end?

The only thing keeping us from
the awareness of Truth,
is the awareness of illusion.

We assume what we think is true, even if it is false. But the Truth of Being cannot come into a mind that holds beliefs opposing its own nature.

It is not that we don't know, but rather that we do. It is our conviction that illusion is Truth and Truth illusion, that keeps us bound to false perception.

The Undoing of Illusion

Illusions are false perceptions. The only way they are undone is by looking at them and judging whether they are based on reality as it is, or as we interpret it to be. But this cannot be done alone, because we made illusions by believing in them. How then can we correct our own mistakes?

We need help in doing this; something beyond ourselves that can decide for us and this comes from the Source of Life, the deeper Self, our Inner Being.

It is our responsibility to recognize when we are unhappy. But it is not for us to find peace ourselves. This is not our work, as we must turn error over to the Greater Self, who alone knows Truth.

There are many names and faces for Inner Being; many ways to reach out and touch that deeper part of our Self. The form we use is irrelevant. It is the willingness that makes the difference; without it the journey can not begin, nor be traveled. In every step we take there is the decision to continue walking.

If all our fear, anger, guilt, despair, unhappiness is who and what we are, we would not seek for change. We would live our lives as miserable creatures, because that is our reality. But that we do, is the recognition there must be a better way to live because we are better than this and it is our Inner Being that is the unseen source of the impulse for greater understanding.

The undoing of illusions is found
on the road to something better.

Throughout history, humankind has developed many traditions, methods, practices, religions, spiritualities, all in an attempt to reach the Higher Self. What works for some may not work for others. Though, it is certain, there is a path for everyone. The forms differ, but the content is always the same. The way lies within.

The higher self is not an old sage we turn to for guidance and wisdom. We are this Self at another level of reality. We don't know this, because awareness is constrained by our intense focus on the physical world. Yet, our Energy comes from this deeper place. To reach it, however, we must be willing to step back and look in another direction.

What compels us to do this? Why would we take our attention away from daily life, to peer into the unknown? Because, we discover, it is our Will.

Finding your Path

For many, the path within begins with the acceptance, something is not working. Whatever we are doing, thinking, perceiving is not bringing us what we want. We are not happy, healthy, successful, peaceful and instead, are conflicted, afraid, angry, guilty, depressed.

Most people, however, seek to make their lives better by trying to adjust circumstances, or worse accept, defeat and drown themselves in negativity. They medicate their pain, live in denial or busy themselves with distraction, all in an attempt to avoid facing the real issue.

But, it is those with courage, who finally come to the realization it is not the world, but it is me that needs to change and more profoundly, that I don't know how to change myself.

There are endless avenues to travel to find greater self-understanding and the way we choose depends on what we think we are.

When we seek answers from the world, we are relegated to that which believes in the world - science, medicine, diet, fitness and an endless variation of ideas that assert it is the body that needs to be saved. For them, the mind is an aspect of the brain and can be treated with drugs. Or what we ingest and eat, the exercise we get, can in some way bring peace and happiness. But it never works because we are just treating the symptoms and not the dysfunction, the effects and not the cause.

In some small measure, science accepts the mind may need some shrinking and offers therapy and counseling as its method.

It can be a good starting point, as it allows an individual to begin looking at themselves safely. Eventually though, if you don't evolve to a higher learning it becomes a trap of self-indulgence, going round and round, but never getting anywhere. Trying to understand ego and its motivations, is like grasping for a balloon that always seems to slip away when reaching for it.

It does not lead to true enlightenment because its basic premise, that the mind is an effect of the body is not true. You cannot heal the nonphysical with anything physical.

The only true path to undoing illusions is at its source - our thought system.

The Correction of Perception

In the mind, healing is not fixing something broken, nor is it repairing its fundamental nature. It is perfect, whole and eternal. There is nothing about Energy itself, that needs to be made right. It simply IS. Yet, it can be misdirected and used to make what is out of accord with Itself and this leads to suffering.

All suffering is the attempt to prove what is false is true and what is illusion is reality. If such a goal were not intolerable, it wouldn't matter. But that it feels so bad in doing it, we are compelled to seek relief.

Healing then, is setting perceptions aright and freeing ourselves from the false beliefs that bring mental despair and instead, experiencing the Joy that is the natural outcome of right thinking.

Perception is corrected by learning to think differently about what we are seeing, since perception is interpreting what we see. The approach best suited for us, is something we can understand and accomplish what speaks to our heart, our intellect and our experience. The specific path we travel reveals itself, when we are ready.

In essence though, all practices are the same, with the same purpose, bringing the same result. That is how we know if we have chosen wisely, does it bring peace?

Inner Peace is the hallmark of Truth and when we are distressed, in conflict or, disturbed to any degree then, our interpretation of events is wrong.

For us, because mind is powerful and belief is strong, changing our own thinking is impossible. We cannot stand on our shoulders to climb out of a hole we've dug too deep, or solve a problem we created by believing in problems.

It is quite obvious why so many have a negative, fatalistic view of life, when confronting themselves with their own unhappiness. They see no hope, believing fully in their hopelessness. But the Universe is far kinder to us and we are never without help.

No one can endure suffering forever. Though our tolerance for pain is enormous, it is not without limit and there comes a point in everyone's life, when they've had quite enough and can endure it no longer.

We will always seek to remedy distress. We fail, however, when we try to do it ourselves. Correcting error, is a process we must undertake with our Greater Self, who alone knows our Reality.

How then do we connect with this unseen Self and have our minds healed?

The first step is ours to take. Without our consent, nothing happens. Things begin to shift, however, when we show the slightest willingness to listen. It is only then, can we open the door to another Voice.

We begin by acknowledging we are not content with our current mental/emotional state and want peace instead.

When the body is confronted with a painful situation, we immediately seek to withdraw from it or flee. It is a natural reaction to put down a burning ember or recoil from a pin prick. It is a protective defense mechanism, built into the human condition.

In the same manner, when the mind is suffering, we also look for relief. But the dilemma we face, is there is no where for it to go. So we attempt many different strategies, to escape ourselves.

It is common for people to medicate themselves through drinking or drugs, thinking by altering the brain's chemistry we can alter our thoughts. Or, putting on a happy face while denying sadness and being distracted by trivial busyness. But these schemes never really accomplish their goal.

The most common approach we use, is the psychological strategy of projection. Instead of saying, I am the cause of my unhappiness, we say my unhappiness is caused by something outside myself. It is not me that is at fault, but you and what you are doing, that makes me feel badly.

The next step develops along the lines of a deeper recognition, that it is not the situation we are in causing us pain, but our judgement of its meaning instead.

A profound shift occurs, when we are willing to accept responsibility for our sight, instead of blaming what we are seeing. This is the beginning of looking within, as we bring ourselves back to the real source of our distress and that is in our minds, not out in the world.

We entrap ourselves in misery, by placing suffering outside us, because we have no control over it and what we cannot control, we cannot change.

Having finally placed the reason for unhappiness within ourselves, we take the final steps towards correction.

It is a powerful statement to accept responsibility for our mental state and while that is a necessary understanding, it is not enough to bring peace. There is no real difference between saying there is something wrong with the world and there is something wrong with me. Both forms of condemnation bring fear, guilt and despair.

Healing, which is changing our thoughts, can only occur when we accept that we are not seeing reality but our belief about reality. Reality is immutable and cannot be changed. But a belief, no matter how strongly felt, is still just an opinion.

With some humility, we accept our perceptions, though believed in, can still be mistaken. Isn't it better that we are mistaken rather than condemned, to be happy then right?

The last step taken is a releasing of our minds and turning over our thinking to a higher level of Being.

We say this to ourselves: As a human being I perceive this one way, but as an Eternal Being I see it another and I want to see this differently. Give me the clarity I need for greater understanding.

Then, we step back and let go, allowing for another perception. It will come as a quiet stream of gentle thoughts bringing with it a new experience, so completely remarkable, it will seem miraculous.

This is the true definition of a miracle, being able to see with Inner Being, what we could not see ourselves. In that moment, we are freed from the chains of suffering that kept us bound to fear, to hatred, lack, limitation and death. We have touched the Divine Within and are raised above the battle ground of human existence.

It is beyond understanding. It is deep. It is what we have been searching for our entire lives. For that one instant, we remember our True Self and find the Joy that is Its gift.

Nothing left to be said. This is the salvation of the world. What more needs to be done? We have found redemption.

Peace is found in the letting go of illusions
and accepting only
what is True is true.

And then we turn our attention back to the world and just as suddenly, we are seeing through the body's eyes again and living in the illusion of mortal existence. All the pain and suffering, returns. But, perhaps not as much. Something in us has shifted. We took a step forward; an inch maybe but still, we moved and what seemed impossible a moment ago, now seems inevitable.

We will forget, but a small part of us of now remembers there is another way of seeing that is kinder and gentler, a way of thinking that is more forgiving and loving. This is a glimmer of hope we can carry with us, wherever we go.

We felt it, that strength. It was profound and we began to wonder why we don't perceive the world this way all the time? Who would not want to be powerful and unlimited? What sane person wants to be weak, angry and downtrodden?

The answer, though hidden, is not surprising. We are not in our right minds when looking through a glass darkly. But, because we have invested so much into thinking life is a certain way, we cannot easily give it up.

Healing can be effortlessly accomplished. We simply recognize when we are unhappy, ask for help and have our errors undone, returning to right perception. But there is one formidable obstacle that stands in our way.

So compelling is the need to have our beliefs proven true, that we will literally sacrifice ourselves and others, on the altar of fear and guilt just to be right.

Though, it is not the Us that is in alignment with Inner Being that offers resistance. Rather, it is the small self who holds to the ego vision of being a separated individual and would establish that as reality.

The ego opposes Inner Being because they are opposites. Our Greater Self is unlimited eternal energy, reaching across the Universe, at One with All That Is.

Ego is in the life of the body, limited, frail, weak, destined to die. Wanting to be separate and apart from its Source, it seeks its own self-sustaining existence.

But, ego is not a being on its own, neither does it have a life outside our minds. It is just an idea of separation we cling to, because we want it to be true. We choose to believe the body is all we are and there is no such thing as the Self. We want to be the sole arbiter of our experience, whose fate we alone decide.

But, like any belief, to continue it must be maintained. If we stop upholding it, it disappears. Only Truth is eternal and needs no support.

Ego then, seeks to prove itself true, for what is true never ends. We are always looking for validation it is real and so, we are right to believe in it.

This is the fundamental conflict all human beings experience in one form or another. In a sense, it is a battle between ego and Spirit, Truth and illusion. It is not a real war, though It can appear that way. Can reality assail itself and remain whole?

Physical life is a constant struggle, when we feel embattled and under siege by something outside ourselves. The journey is fraught with roadblocks we have placed in our way. The Universe is not against us and there is nothing stopping us from realizing our Eternal Nature. But that we are completely unaware of it, should tell us something is amiss.

To become Enlightened is to gain understanding. But enlightenment is not learning anything we don't already know. It is unlearning every false idea we have about the world and ourselves, that keeps us from that knowledge.

Our minds are dark, until illumination comes. But illusions will not go unless we look at them, for it is by not looking at them they remain.

We cannot see the Light
until we look at the darkness and
recognize it, for what it is.

This is the road taken,
by all seekers of Truth.

A Sixth Truth

Darkness and Light

The world is a dark place for many and it is a darkness that covers our eyes so we cannot see, even though Light is all around us. What we perceive instead, are shadows that move from here to there and appear to live but have no life. Quietly then, we despair, having placed faith in the faithless. But Truth, is always hopeful and it is in our hopelessness we lack understanding.

In feverish nightmares, we fear an evil that hates all which is good; horrifying figures lurking in the shadows, whose bony fingers reach out, grasping at our throats; their snarling mouths eager to devour our very lives; their one purpose, to destroy.

Humanity has long imagined monsters that roam the night, rampaging as they go; serpents swimming in murky seas drowning helpless victims and dark lords who wage war on the meek, in their quest for dominion over all that lives. The countless stories of the battle between good and evil is legend - a common theme found in every culture, of every age.

We think, because this idea is so ancient and so often told, it must be true. Yet, such beings do not exist and there is no place called hell where devils dwell and lost souls burn in the eternal fires of damnation.

There are no dark forces or sinister energies prowling the Universe; no vampires, werewolves, or demons who prey on humankind. It is all a story, a dream, a mad projection by those chained to fear and guilt, that what it is within can be seen without, in hopes of making themselves safe from their own dark thoughts.

But darkness has no properties of its own. It is not of malevolent intent or has destructive influence. It is not a power that rises from the depths to oppose goodness, overshadowing what is beautiful and killing those who are innocent. Of itself, it's nothing.

In all its seemingly terrible forms and evil connotations, it is no more than the absence of Light.

Light in physical terms, is a movement of energy that reveals the terrains of our world. Without it, we could not survive or grow, gather materials to make tools or fashion clothes, hunt for food or collect water. We would quickly fall into a ravine and be destroyed. There would be no invention, no families, no civilizations – there could be no human race.

Non-physically, Light is also a movement of Energy, but as Awareness. It reveals the inner landscapes of our mind. Without It, we could not know our own Nature or our Self.

Light is Awareness,
as darkness is unknowing.
Light is Understanding,
as darkness is ignorance.

Darkness seems real to those who believe in it, for it is the power of belief that gives it a reality. Though, its influence is limited to minds who uphold it and while they dwell in the shadows of ignorance, they can perceive nothing else.

In the mind, darkness is not an unseeing blackness. It can seem vibrant and alive, powerful and all-encompassing. Rather, it is seeing what is not there in Truth - the perception of illusions.

Within itself, it appears logical and sane and while we live our lives with false thoughts, we will believe they are true and suffer out of allegiance to them.

We know our minds need to be lit, when we are not at peace or happy because both Peace and Happiness come from the Light of Understanding. But, if we are ever to live a full, meaningful existence then, we must confront our misthoughts and see them for what they are, not what we want them to be.

The Dark Side of Human Existence

We all have a dark side. It is an integral part of the human experience. No matter, how kind, religious, caring, pious, enlightened and loving we think we are, still, there is that part of us that dwells in darkness. To deny this, is to be trapped in a life not truly lived, with a potential unfulfilled.

Our purpose here, is the healing of our minds; reconciling the good with the bad, the right with the wrong and what is true with what is false. While we are eager to recognize positive thoughts, we are not so willing to acknowledge negative thinking and would rather it not exist. But, it is only by embracing all of our self we become whole and it is only in wholeness we understand our true Nature.

The journey to the Light is through the darkness.

We are all terrified of the dark inside ourselves. We imagine it to be the greatest evil and if we looked within, we'd find the worst kind of sinner, a murderer who wants to kill the world and eventually themselves.

In a sense this is true, for such thinking is destructive. But what is eternal cannot destroy or be destroyed. So, it must be something else.

Dark thoughts are kept alive, by being hidden in unawareness. We think them, but don't necessarily recognize their meaning. We assume we know and so, our deepest beliefs are never brought into question. If we truly want to find peace, however, we must look at all that causes us pain and seek to have it healed.

Fear

Everyone experiences fear and more than they realize. There is fear that is clearly felt - your heart races, your breathing is fast and your body goes numb.

Mostly though, it goes unrecognized, like a mist engulfing you, clouding your vision and covering your mind with a subtle dread. Suddenly, the bright day is dimmed and life seems hopeless, but you don't know why.

Fear is pervasive, with many forms. It can appear as something good to those who advocate for it, or something detrimental. But, it will always have a negative impact on your life. It is the great enslaver, secretly keeping you bound to helplessness, for only the weak and vulnerable can be afraid. Like any emotion, it is the result of our thinking.

Thoughts that lead to fear are varied and seemingly unrelated. Yet, they all share a common meaning. What creates fear in anyone is always the same. In some manner, we perceive ourselves as being threatened.

Physical harm is obvious and being frightened is a natural outcome of thinking our body is in danger. But, what is not so clearly recognized, are those existential threats to our mental/emotional well-being that can dominate our experience.

Fundamentally, all fear is a consequence of attack. Whether being attacked by something outside of us. Or, of us attacking ourselves.

I am afraid when I have bills I cannot pay.

I am afraid of driving at night.

I am afraid of being sued.

I am afraid of bugs.

I am afraid of heights.

I am afraid of speaking in public.

I am afraid of being alone.

There is an unending list of things to be afraid of in this world. But, as with all emotion, it is a result of our belief.

I am afraid when I have bills to pay, because if I don't pay my bills, I believe something bad will occur.

I am afraid of driving at night, because I can't see very far and I believe I could hit something or something will hit me and I might get seriously hurt.

I am afraid of being sued, because if I lose I would owe someone money and they would come after me.

I am afraid of bugs, because I believe they would crawl on me and bite me and I could get sick.

I am afraid of heights, because I believe I could fall to the ground and get badly injured.

I am afraid of speaking in public, because I believe if I stutter or misspeak people will laugh at me and I would feel embarrassed.

I am afraid of being alone, because if something happened to me, there would be no one there to help.

Take any fear and within it you will see some form of attack. As it has been often repeated though, it is not the circumstance itself that causes fear. It is the meaning we give it.

When our bills go unpaid, we feel afraid because in this world there are negative consequences. The electric company can turn the power off. Without power there is no light or heat. We can't live in a dark house. We could freeze to death.

But what is the real threat here? Is it not having electricity? Because people have lived for eons before its development. No, it is the belief that our bodies cannot survive in this world without it, that is the source of fear.

Fear is very logical. Looking at the outer world, who wouldn't be afraid of negative circumstances? Who would be happy having the heat turned off? Or, are at peace with bill collectors knocking on the door?

On the surface fear is sane. It is only the deeper you go into its thought system where it becomes illogical.

The basis for all feelings, are the underlying beliefs that provide a framework for our perceptions the interpretation given to events, whose foundation is the idea of who and what we are.

If fear is an effect of attack, then when afraid, we are perceiving our nature and our self, as something that can be changed or diminished, making us less.

Fear comes from the perceived defeat of our Will.

If our will is to live, then we will be fearful of any situation we believe opposes our desire to continue living. But, our life is not just the body, it is also the mind. So, even if our physical existence is not in jeopardy, we can still be afraid, thinking our self-identity is being assailed.

Why would I be terrified of performing or speaking in front of a crowd of people? I might be pelted with tomatoes but nothing that would send me to the hospital. It is that I believe people will think poorly of me and my self-worth will be lessened by their rejection. Further, that somehow my life depends on their approval.

Fear's deepest belief is that our will can be defeated by something outside our Self. That is why it feels so overwhelming. Yet, we can never overcome our anxieties, by placing their source beyond our control. It is only by taking responsibility for our emotional experience, that we can ever change it, for the better.

Understanding leads to peace. To understand fear then, we must bring it back to its cause and look at it in the Light of Clarity, not once, but each time it comes to haunt us.

The Causes of Fear

Fear is seen as both unbidden and unstoppable. It's major premise is the idea, that it comes to us against our will.

**Fear is all about what we don't want,
not what we do.**

We have no power in fear, for it is the belief in powerlessness. Who, standing in strength, can be afraid of anything? It is only in the perception that we are weak and vulnerable can we feel endangered.

I am walking down the street, late at night and approached by a stranger with a knife demanding money. For most people, that would be a terrifying situation.

But what if I had a gun, would I still be concerned? Or, if I were wearing a suit of armor? More radically, what if I didn't care about money and was glad to give it to them, seeing them as desperate and in need of help. Wouldn't I feel compassion instead, that someone was in such need, they had to resort to mugging another person for a few dollars?

Fear is two-fold. It is being confronted by something that opposes our will and secondly, believing we are unable to meet that threat.

Though an egregious act may seem to warrant it, it is still our interpretation that determines how we feel. Regardless of outer conditions and events, fear is a feeling, not a reality.

**Fear is in the mind,
not the world.**

We can just as easily let go of trepidation as any other negative emotion. It is all a matter of seeing things differently. The great difficulty, however, is that our Nature is immutable. We always seek Life and resist what goes against our Will.

So, does that mean we have to be frightened of opposing conditions? No. It is not being challenged that creates anxiety, but the idea of being defeated. If all belief is really self-belief, then the foundation of every fear we have, is some negative concept we hold about ourself.

The question we must ask ourselves is: What do we believe about who we are that causes us to be afraid?

For us, we experience fear every day and so, assume it is part of the natural order. We cannot imagine being completely free of it, even the smallest anxiety of going outside on a rainy day without an umbrella.

Fearlessness, we imagine, is a state only attained by those with super powers who can be unmoved by threatening conditions. But, there is no fear in Truth and when we are afraid we are not living truly.

In all its forms and manifestations, it is founded on the fundamental concept, there is something outside of me more powerful than I am, that opposes my will. In this view of myself, what am I then and what is against me?

To be independent of anything, means you are separate from it and being separate stand in opposition; only what is joined together is One and shares the same life.

In this world, what is apart from everything? What survives by itself and competes with everyone else, for the same resources to live? Is it not the body?

When we see ourselves as merely physical beings, fear is inevitable and if that is our sole reality, it can never be overcome. We are fated to walk the Earth, bound to a certain apprehension that may be abated, but never goes away.

But there is always hope in Truth, for in it lies the recognition, we are more than just the human we see, and are an unseen Energy that transcends mortal existence.

Fear is threat but only bodies can attack one another. The great paradox here, is, though we feel it in the body, that is not where it is created. Rather, its source is in the mind and so, if we choose, it can be undone from within.

It is the mind that creates fear
and it is the Mind
that undoes it.

Fear and our self-concept

If trepidation were caused by outer circumstances, we would forever be doomed to despair, because we cannot control the world. But what we can command is our perception, whose founding principle is the self-concept.

The idea of our self is different then the Truth of Self. We do not live with Knowledge, but with belief. It is an inherent aspect of the human experience, that we look outward for reality and this makes us susceptible to illusions, from which all fear is born.

To perceive correctly is to be in alignment with our Nature. When we are afraid of anything, it is because we are going against our own will and seeing ourselves as weak and vulnerable. But, that is the sad consequence of identifying with the destructible.

Fears are lies we tell ourselves.

Fear never speaks the truth of what we are. It always speaks to our illusions. In that moment then, when we are terrified by some perceived threat, we must turn to our Greater Self and ask for clarity. "Is this really what I am? Or am I something else more powerful, more secure, more supported? Is this my Truth or is Peace?"

We stand in the middle of our mind, looking out or looking within. The part that sees itself as a body, we call the ego. What knows itself as Energy we call Spirit.

Spirit is a Oneness that is undivided and so, cannot experience fear. It is but our ego, that is ever afraid.

When we feel the slightest apprehension, the smallest dread, or the tiniest unease, it is because we have chosen to identify with the ego-body illusion.

We perceive ourselves as standing alone in the world, battling for our meager portion of what is needed to live. Fear comes from nowhere else but being separate bodies, each vying to survive.

It is a wrong minded attempt to perceive ourselves as limited by the physical - being weak, unable to defend ourselves and destined to die.

It is darkness, because it does not reflect the light of understanding that we are all Energy joined together as One.

On appearance, who can deny the body its vulnerability and its death? No one. So worry appears justified. Truth, however, is not about what seems real, but what is real.

The issue in life is not fear itself, but what it represents. It is just a feeling and like all feelings, are fleeting. They do not exist by themselves, but are caused by thoughts. Thoughts too are transitory. They come and go, so often and persistent they seem to have a greater reality then they actually do. True power though, lies with the Mind, where all emotional experience originates and is felt.

Mind creates reality. It is where we exist and have our being. What it makes it supports, even upholding its miscreations, for that is the very nature of energy, in its unending quest to extend itself.

From the Nonphysical came the world and out of the world arose the body and the ego. By projecting ourselves outward, we believe we are outside our Self and look to daily life for experiences that prove this is true.

What then serves the purpose of establishing our identity as the separated ego self, except fear? It teaches us, we are vulnerable and under attack and isn't this what a body is? It is the evidence we need, to continue believing in the physical.

Our ego actively pursues feeling beseiged. It reinforces our conviction, we have an individual life, apart from everyone else that needs to be defended. When it is said, fear is a choice, this is what is meant.

It doesn't seem sane to want to be afraid, because we think it is something actively avoided. Yet, it is precisely this logic that keeps it in place. Regardless, if we recognize it or not, fear is an election. We decide to believe, we are what we are not and experience the results of that decision.

The problem of fear

We may well ask ourselves, what is the problem? Why not just accept it as part of human existence? Why try to overcome it? And the answer is simple. It doesn't bring us peace.

We recognize at some level, it is not what we want and yet, we continue to advocate for it. So, why do we listen to our fears, knowing they makes us unhappy?

Fear comes in a way that seems honorable, like a faithful friend, looking out for our interests. So, we hear its council. But, when we begin to look more closely, its edges begin to unravel, the mist that obscures it fades and finally, we see it with clarity.

Fear is self-deception

Fear has many faces. Some are dreadful and easily recognized, with lips on fire, threatening fangs dripping; a terrible edifice bathed in blood. Others are sweeter and more obscure, smiling and harmless like a kitten. It can appear as a monster overly vicious or timid and shy. It is the great deceiver, for underneath is hidden its true intent.

Many of us think fear is a good thing. It is protective and cares for our safety. It wants to protect us from harm. Without it, we would run into speeding traffic, or haul ourself off a cliff.

It is oh so kindly, in a small voice that quietly whispers in our ear, don't do this, don't do that, we could get hurt. We might be disappointed, or laughed at and rejected. It just wants what is best.

Who can resist the call of Love? So we take heed, abiding its dictates and delude ourselves into thinking we have made a wise decision.

Fear is a wolf in sheep's clothing. It comes speaking the language of love, all the while, condemning us to death and despair. Its motives would seem our protection and yet, we never consider if we actually need to be protected.

In accepting fear's premise, by choosing to follow our fears, we declare ourselves to be both powerless and worthless. Is this something Love would proclaim?

Fear is not your friend

Fear and the unfulfillment of will

Some mornings we wake up and are afraid, but don't know why. There is not an obvious reason and yet we still tremble in the dark of uncertainty.

We're at work and overcome with panic, as though there is something terribly wrong; at home on the couch and feel a certain dread of being taken to task for not doing what is important. So, we look around for what is missing, but nothing seems out of place.

This vague foreboding creeps up in quiet moments and for a brief instant, we feel terrified by an unseen force waiting the opportunity to strike. We look out the window, anticipating a knock on the front door, and wonder what have we done, to be pursued by the Universe? Still we find no answer.

Fear is largely subconscious. We feel it but cannot see a cause; its source is hidden from our awareness. It comes unknowingly, when what we think and believe contradicts our Self.

We exist because we were created and what is created serves a purpose. When we are not true to our function, we are haunted by a sense of unfulfillment, that manifests as anxiety and despair.

In each moment, we are seeking to be happy. But, if every decision we make is meant to fulfill our will, how can it go unfulfilled? If fear does not bring peace, why do we choose it?

The mind that is concentrated on physical existence believes in the body and the ego. So naturally, whatever reinforces that view we pursue. Strangely enough, we believe fear supports our will.

What is wanted also implies what is unwanted. In the same manner, if fear is all about what we don't want, it also speaks to what we do.

When we are afraid, we are stating this is not our will and by consequence, implying what is. So, we believe fear validates what we actually seek.

We cling to fear out of the erroneous concept, we can get what we want through the denial of what we don't want. But, that is not how the mind works.

Fear is not the denial of unfulfillment,
it is the denial of will.

Mind is energy and what we think about manifests, whether we desire it or not. Choosing to be afraid cannot bring us where we need to go. It is a false door in an empty room, leading nowhere and worse, it keeps us from following the right path.

Letting go of fear

Reason would tell us, it is not productive and yet our mind is constantly thinking thoughts that produces fear. It seems a mystery to us, why we do this, even though at another level, we know better. Still, we can't seem to stop ourselves.

But, there is a reason even in this. The ego, out of self-interest, would convince us, fear is not a choice at all, being unwanted that it is caused by something outside ourselves we cannot change. In this view, it is unalterable.

But Truth would say, every perception is still a choice and even though we cannot control outer events, we can decide how we see them and therefore, experience them.

We will never redeem our ego's use of fear, because its continued existence depends on it. The only true way to overcome it then, is for us to be willing to see things differently.

Fear is the dragon of the mortal mind,
standing at the gate to Heaven.
It is the whisper of another life
that cannot be lived, only imagined.
Or dreamt of, in feverish dreams
and where lies our guilt.

Guilt

It can be said, if we suffer in life from anything it is guilt. But it is not just about doing wrong, it is a more pervasive sense of being wrong.

Guilt is predicated on the idea we can harm someone or something and make them less take; away their value and purpose by defeating their will.

On the surface, guilt is a sense of regret; of doing what we would undo if we could; take back harsh words spoken in anger; repair a broken relationship over a misunderstanding.

On another level, it is less specific, more general and encompassing. It spreads out like a shadow covering your eyes with a looming blackness that seems impenetrable. It is a dread that is terrible to feel.

Guilt is always attended by fear, because it is based on an attack. In this world of cause and effect, we expect consequences for our actions and aren't the guilty punished? Isn't karma, what goes around comes around? The anticipation of reprisal always make us afraid.

But, there is a deeper foreboding that comes not from actions, but beliefs in who and what we are.

To attack someone, not with the body but the mind, means we judge them to be wrong or less valued. So, we see them without Love. But, since what we give we receive, we also judge ourselves by the same measure, though we keep this price hidden from our awareness.

When we are unloving to another, we believe we have betrayed love in our Self, by declaring ourselves to be an unloving person.

If Love is our True nature, then by accepting ourselves as guilty we are denying our Greater Self. So we go from doing wrong to being wrong. In guilt then, we believe we have somehow changed our own nature and are no longer what we were created to be.

Guilt is the denial of Self.

Is it not terrifying to deny our own reality? What can the result be but feeling lost, alone and depressed. But like fear, guilt is a choice and also like fear, we see guilt as a good thing.

In our world, if we do something that seems to hurt another and we show no remorse, we're considered to be a heartless sociopath without a conscience. So guilt appears to be loving, because it says it wants to undo the harm that was done.

But guilt is another devious pretense. We think it is caring, when it is not.

Guilt is an illusion

It is true, to feel guilt over anything is to have regret and this we interpret to mean, now we somehow care. But, underneath this façade, is a more insidious idea that we have attacked someone and changed their value and worth.

If you went on a tirade denouncing someone and they laughed in response, would you feel badly about what you said? Probably not.

But, if they broke down in tears, then you might, thinking you took away their self-worth; by laughing they have rejected your view, by crying they accepted it and both are deluded into believing we can change a person's value, through condemnation.

Guilt is based on the premise we have the power to alter reality by judging against it. But, it is only the arrogance of the ego that assumes this is possible and so it is just ego that can feel guilty, for spirit knows no such deception.

For us, we find guilt intolerable because it goes against our very nature. But, nevertheless we believe it as a valid response and uphold it, wanting it to be true. Though we don't consciously acknowledge this, it does serve a purpose.

There is a desperate war against the Universe to prove the separated self is true and we are convinced of its reality through fear and guilt.

When we perceive ourselves as being an unloving person, we think we have changed our eternal nature, which is Love. If Love is Oneness, then in being guilty, we must be no longer part of that Oneness. Isn't this exactly what ego is?

Guilt proves the ego real.

Its purpose is not love, nor its goal. Rather, it wears a mask, disguising itself in beneficence and we go along singing praise to noble guilt. But it is all an illusion, a trick of the mind meant to mislead.

We fail to recognize we are lost in darkness and the path leads not to redemption but crucifixion, for though it seems to be a call for love, it really is the call for death.

But would you follow, seeing with clarity it does not fulfill your will? Nor make you happy or bring you peace? Then it cannot be the Truth, no matter the testimony or how sweet the melody that is played.

Guilt is not Love.

Anger

We can see anger as positive or negative. Someone has righteous anger over injustice, or they have anger issues. Depending on what it is used for, determines what it is. But, at its core it is the same.

Anger is a form of protection; a defense against fear and guilt. It is an attempt to get rid of both, by projecting them outward onto someone or something else, making them fearful and guilty instead.

We think anger is a show of strength, because it is founded in attack and we see attack as power. But it is really a demonstration of weakness. We could never be angry, if we were not first afraid.

While getting angry may feel good in the moment, it does not accomplish the goal it seeks. Its purpose is to make you safer, more empowered, more valued. How then does attacking another achieve this? It really doesn't.

We cannot change another's mind through psychological violence. By doing so, we simply reinforce the source of anger in ourself. But, like guilt, it is only effective if someone else is willing to agree. What if they don't?

On many of his long travels, one day Buddha arrived in a small town. He sat down in front of a large crowd and started teaching. Everyone listened intently, except for one young man in the back, who started heckling him. "You are a liar and a fake," he shouted.

But, Buddha did not respond and kept speaking. This infuriated the man further. So, he shouted even louder. Again, the Buddha calmly continued. Finally, the man could no longer take being ignored and rushed to the front in rage.

But the crowd stopped him and were about to beat him, when the Buddha said, let the man come forward. He then asked him a simple question.

"If you buy a gift and present it to me, but I refuse to accept it, who does the gift belong to?"

The man thought for a minute, and responded, "It would still belong to me."

Then the Buddha said, "By the same measure, when you try to give me your anger and I do not take it from you, it is still yours, not mine and you continue to suffer over having it."

Suddenly, the man understood, he only caused himself harm by being angry. He bowed to the Buddha and sat down, grateful for being freed of that suffering.

What if we did succeed in changing someone's position through anger? We may think we get what we want, but that quickly turns to guilt, over having attacked someone and thinking we defeated their will.

Anger has limited usefulness. Ultimately, it does us more harm then good. It will always lead to negative experience. Why use it then, when there are more fruitful approaches that yield greater results?

Hatred

Hatred is the fire of separation fueled by anger. Its founding principle is otherness, for we only hate what we think is unlike ourself.

We when perceive difference, we can see it through the eyes of Love or the blindness of fear.

Love knows no hatred, because its foundation is Oneness, where all things share the same Life.

Fear can only hate, because its base is division, where things exist unto themselves and stand against each other.

Whatever it be, a person, place, thing, event, condition, we will hate what shares not our Will.

Hatred then, like all illusions, is based on false beliefs, for in all the Universe there exists nothing we are not connected to; in the entire world, there is everything we are joined with.

There is another hatred, more obscure, yet as destructive. Within each of us, is a place where hate abides and it is not the hatred of what is outside, but what is within.

We despise ourselves and know it not, when we are sick or fail at something we want to do. It comes disguised as self-criticism and thought to be ennobling, an expression of humility. It is not considered good manners to love yourself or think yourself great.

Self-hatred though, is a dark cornerstone in the foundation of ego. It is the separation of our self from our Self. It is the supreme contradiction, for how can what we are, oppose what we want? But isn't this the basis of all sickness? Isn't this what depression is and mental illness? How is it that we can turn against ourself, except in hate.

Evil

The belief in evil is humanity's attempt to understand how it is possible to live in a loving Universe and still encounter horrifying nightmares.

Evil would stand as the opposite to all that is good. It seeks destruction, not creation, ruin not abundance, death not life.

But such a thing can only be imagined, for it is impossible Life could create its own destruction. It is a silly child's dream, that somehow Creation can be overthrown by itself; that sanity can turn to madness and Love can become fear.

In our world, the evil that is thought to be done, is not seen as wicked by those who do it, but part of their own quest for survival. In war, actions are justified because in their minds, it serves a greater purpose.

To kill another person, or millions, no matter the reason cannot be seen as good. But what is not good comes from the darkness of ignorance, not a thing of its own. Is dying an evil in itself? For people die everyday and though mourned, it is considered part of life.

The battle between good and evil is a prevalant theme in every story that has a hero or a villan and so, there has to be an enemy that can be defeated. But, we never ask where such a dark force or dark mind comes from.

Who is the creator of evil? Surely, it cannot be the All That Is, would give life to what would overthrow its Own Will. It must be us then, that thinks it so.

But, evil is simply the failure to take responsibility for our own dark thoughts and keep them hidden, for when darkness is brought to light, it is seen as a contradiction and what contradicts itself cannot stand.

If such malevolence existed, it would have to follow its nature, to beget as it was begotten. What is evil seeks desolation, not expansion. If it was created, in that same moment, it would turn back and destroy itself, for only what seeks Life, can continue to live and only Love seeks Life.

Death

As Life is beginning, death is ending - it is the idea things begin and end. There is a starting point and a stopping point, beyond which nothing continues.

In the physical world, this is true, everything here that lives dies. Though we try to deny it, shrink from it, run from it, we cannot escape it. Death comes for all. It is a reality that can never be undone. It is what the Earth is, the mortal realm.

But do we die because our life has run out? As if there was a finite amount and when finally depleted, we cease to exist? If death is real, then what is life and where does it come from?

The body is the vessel for physical existence. We keep it going by eating, drinking, breathing, sleeping, but still we don't know how it lives. If Life is such a mystery, how then are we so sure what death is?

It is because that is what we see and when the body stops, it shrinks into nothingness, leaving but the remnants of its bones behind. Perhaps to endure a little longer, but then turning back to dust over time. What though, of the mind that gave the body direction? Where did that go?

Where do the dying go?
Do they disappear like melted snow?
Or as paper
in a magician's hand,
folded smaller and smaller
until vanished,
into thin air?

If we are the body, then we have but a temporary existence that in the end leads to nowhere and all we did in between was for nothing.

If death is real, life is meaningless

Life has no meaning in death. It is just a spinning wheel going round and round without a goal; begun by chance or accident, it has no soul. It has no function.

The mortal self hears the beat of the humdrum world, banging in a monotonous tone. Stroke by stroke, it pulls the oars of the galley ship that sails to oblivion, a slave to the cruel master Death. It can but mourn its fate, while it seems to live awhile, ever shrouded in the pall of doom.

If death is real, there is no true hope, joy is a delusion, peace a fantasy and love a dream.

Yet, every day we wake with the promise of life shining before us. There is something within that keeps us going. Perhaps it is not understood, but It is no idle wish. It is a reality.

It speaks of what lies beyond our vision; what is underneath the pillars of the Earth; what lies behind the veil, that seems to separate physical from nonphysical.

Life is Energy. Energy cannot die, nor be diminished. But it can and does change form. It can manifest in matter and unmanifest as easily. Though its essence is eternal.

As a process, death is merely the movement of energy away from conditional existence. It is a change of direction of eternal Mind.

The mind cannot die, but it can believe in death and this is the source of all sorrow in human existence.

There is death,
but of the body
not the Mind.

The Belief in Death

The mind is powerful and what it believes in, it holds to be true and fully experiences the results of that assertion. We live what we believe, whether it is true or not.

For us death is real. We see it with our eyes, touch it with our hands, smell it with our nose. We don't know with certainty, what happens when a person dies and in not knowing we doubt anything else exists.

So, the idea of death lies hidden in the subconscious, being too dreadful to dwell openly in our daily thoughts, but still having a profound influence on everything we think. There is nothing we do, it touches not.

Consider what death is and we can see its gaunt hands shaping our experience.

Death is the final and complete defeat of our will.

Death is the cause of every unhappy thought and feeling we ever have. It stands against us, more powerful than our desire to continue living; a terrible enemy that cannot be overcome. What can we feel facing such adversity, except a hopelessness so deep, it is a bottomless pit of despair, a depression so black no light could ever enter.

What is fear but being attacked by something greater than ourself? And what is greater than us but death? It is the power we think, comes to overthrow our will.

Guilt is believing we have condemned another and lessened their meaning. What makes all things meaningless, if not the loss of what is valued?

Anger would be a protection against threat and what is our greatest threat, if not the end of our life?

Hatred is for that which does not share our will. If our will is to live then, is not what is hated what would defeat us?

Evil opposes goodness and what is good but Life? What stands against Life if not death?

Death is darkness
and the source of all dark thoughts.

In one form or another, every dark thought we have about ourself or another comes from death. It is the cause and fear, guilt, anger, hate, despair, depression, hopelessness, meaningless are its effects.

Death may seem to be a physical act. But all action is an expression of something deeper. The Mind precedes the body and its thoughts exist non-physically, before their physical manifestation.

Death is a belief.

Though we watch our physical structures disintegrate, never to return as proof of our mortality, it is still just a concept. Death is an idea of destruction held in the mind, that eternal energy can be destroyed and what is never ending, can have an end.

Each belief we hold is a choice, even believing in death is a decision. We could, just as firmly and with greater conviction not believe it. But, we choose to accept what perception shows because, as with every other dark idea, it serves a purpose.

Who thinks death can achieve its goals? A murderer, serial killer, a warrior, one seeking revenge, a dark lord? Or perhaps all of us, in some way.

No one wants their demise to be true and yet, we continue to assert its reality for a reason. The part of us that understands itself as energy has no such motivation. It is that which thinks it is a body that looks to its ending.

While death would defeat life, we still use it as a weapon against Truth, for how can Eternal Beings die? So, it upholds the belief we are not our Self.

Death and the self

Death is an idea that takes many forms. We maintain it, without recognizing how.

In all fear, the ego whispers of ruin.

In all guilt, the ego calls for punishment.

In all anger, the ego speaks of killing.

In all hatred, the ego shouts for murder.

In all evil is the hand of death.

We are all murderers without knowing it; all killers without understanding what killing is.

In death, what ends but being? We think the body is our self, so when it ceases to breathe, only that we call our end. But while we live in the physical world, we experience it day to day, not realizing that is what it is.

Death of self is not just the form, it is also the content, the concept we hold of ourselves in our minds. It is this self we perceive as threatened by thoughts and judgments and the condemnations of others. Even though we are physically safe from harm, we can still be terrified.

Why is an insult like a dagger in the back? Many people have been assaulted just for looking at someone the wrong way. It attests to the Truth, the ego is just a concept of who and what we are and not a reality.

Ideas are energy and energy is never static, it is always in motion. The concepts we hold in our minds must be sustained, by extending outward and strengthened through sharing. So, when others don't share our view of ourself, we think it is less valid and less real. This we perceive as threat and respond accordingly.

By the same consequence, we believe we can lessen someone's self by attacking them non-physically. Essentially though, isn't this what killing and murder is?

Whenever we look at someone without love or compassion, we see their death before us, because we do not seek to support their life.

When we judge another as guilty or wrong, we believe justice demands their punishment and sentences them to damnation.

In anger and hatred we see an enemy at the gates and would defend ourselves by destroying them.

We see death as power, more powerful than life itself the hand of destruction is greater than the hand of creation. It is the same illusion that thinks hate, anger and attack are stronger than love, compassion and kindness.

To understand this belief we have to understand what the ego is, for it is the ego that supports it.

The ego has no being of its own. Its life is in the mind, whose energy comes from the Greater Self. The ego cannot create anything by itself. But it can and does foster beliefs that distort the Truth.

The ego uses death as proof of its independent existence, by declaring it can undo the Will of the Universe. The ego's one goal, in all things, is always separation. Understanding this purpose, we can then see what dark thoughts are really for.

Fear, guilt, anger, hatred and everything else that brings unhappiness, all attest to the reality of destruction. If death is the opposite of life and life is Oneness, then death creates separation.

Death is a hammer,

the ego bangs on the door of oneness,

trying to splinter it into a million pieces.

But, we need to remember, the ego is Us. It is we, who continue to listen when it speaks and it is we who want to be this self and not our Self. For then, we have our own life we direct and control. Or so it would seem.

Negative Thinking

This is one of life's greatest mysteries. Why we think negative thoughts, not about others, but about ourself. Most especially, when beliefs are chosen.

Why would we willingly believe in what clearly makes us unhappy, opposes our will and would destroy us if given the opportunity?

Beliefs are developed over time and as we grow, are formed in childhood. At a certain level they are adopted and never questioned. So, unless as adults, we challenge them, they remain to determine our experience.

For some, there is not much they can do to change and are forever bound by the negative images they hold. But for others, there is everything they can do. It is only a matter of willingness, to dare open the door to greater self-understanding.

Who does not have negative thoughts about themselves and their life? Even the most rich and successful, most accomplished people are haunted by darkness. It is unavoidable because it is endemic to being human.

Negative thinking seems more powerful than we are. We cannot stop ourselves from doing it and are always imagining the worst thing possible. Our own mind seems to go against us and be our greatest enemy.

But the mind was created only to serve Being, not turn on itself. So it cannot be Mind that is the cause. It does what it does, which is continually offer up its contents for our acceptance. Thoughts are not thrust upon us by an outside agency. We still choose what we think, even if we don't want to think it. Ultimately, we are in command.

Why though, do we continue to allow ourselves to think negative thoughts? The only reason is, because we believe they are true.

Negative thoughts are all the same, that somehow our will can be defeated. But for this to happen, there must be something that opposes us and seeks our downfall.

We don't challenge this premise, because underneath we want to stand apart from everyone and everything else. But, to do this, we have to create the appearance of opposition. We have to make the Universe into an adversary.

This is the fundamental delusion behind all darkness, that we have a different life from All That Is. So, we cling to negative thoughts, in hopes of protecting the belief in separation from being corrected. Doesn't our thoughts demonstrate we are the thing we think? Negative thoughts prove we are different from what is good.

If I am in conflict, how can I be what brings peace? If I am lacking, how can I be what creates abundance? If I am afraid, how can I be what gives Love?

We made the ego by wanting it to be our Self; to be a thing other than the Oneness we were created to be. We sought to be our own Creator, to take the place of God and gain attributes we do not possess. Ego is all about power and in Unity, we think we are powerless.

Here is the secret motivation, behind all we do and seek, but would hold back from our awareness, to keep division going. For if we did look at it in the Light of Clarity, it might not seem so desirable or wanted, having failed to bring us what we sought.

Then, what would we do, but be compelled to have all of our illusions undone. But, this requires great willingness to admit we have been misled and have the courage to see what has not been seen before.

It is the journey we would take, from the shadows into the Light, to save ourselves from suffering and save the world from pain.

The Light

The Light has come, for all who dwell in darkness, drown in misery and haunted by terrible thoughts. It is here, but how do we see it if we are blind? How do we understand, if we are lost in the lies we tell ourselves?

There is a path we walk, on gentler slopes and set sail on calmer seas. It begins with the recognition we are not happy, but need to be. We just want to wake up to peace. We can't endure being afraid anymore. We are tired of the unrelenting march of struggle and dissatisfaction with life. There has to be a better way, otherwise it is all so meaningless.

We are blessed but know it not. It is time to reclaim the glory of our Self and hear the Voice that speaks of Eternity. Today we will hear the Truth.

Illusions will not leave our minds, while we think them real. Yet, it is in clarity, we learn to see what they are and are willing to let them go.

It is perilous though, to wander in unawareness alone. Walking through darkness without a Light to guide our way, is to risk falling into the pit of despair; thinking we can solve problems on our own, is the same as pretending we created ourselves and know the meaning and purpose of our Life.

We can only see truly with the Greater Self, for the ego knows nothing, being a denial of Knowledge.

The Forgiveness of illusions

In darkness, we condemn ourselves to death by believing we are a body destined to die. But we cannot overcome this judgement, nor pay the price it demands, through punishment or sacrifice. It is only in forgiveness, we can atone for our errors.

Forgiveness though, does not make illusions real and then undoes them, for what has reality cannot be undone. Rather, it no longer upholds false ideas and accepts, only what is true is true.

If clarity comes from Inner Being, then forgiveness is looking at Life through the eyes of eternity and having our perceptions corrected by our Greater Self. It is seeing things differently.

How do we know what is false and needs correcting? By the way our perception causes us to feel.

To find happiness, we must learn to forgive everything that makes us unhappy, brings us fear and guilt and causes us pain and suffering.

Perception is constant. We are either condemning or forgiving, limiting ourselves to the body or acknowledging the Spirit, There is no compromise in this. Death is not partial but complete, as is salvation.

The process always begins with some form of pain; maybe physical, but more so, emotional. We are suffering and recognize something is wrong. We are afraid, distraught, angry, enraged, depressed.

For a moment, unnoticed in time, we stand at a fork in the road. Do we accept our negative thinking and continue on, as we have always done. Or, do we decide it has not led us where we needed to go. We sought for joy, to feel loved, appreciated and safe, but found despair and unworthiness instead.

Perhaps finally, we are willing to accept our approach doesn't work. We don't know how to find peace and it is at this crossroads, the direction of our life can change.

Words mean nothing.

Intent says everything.

DARKNESS AND LIGHT

When we turn to Inner being for help, it doesn't matter how we do it, only we do it sincerely. We can sit in prayer for hours and receive no answer; meditate for weeks and come to no greater understanding. But, one instant of total willingness can bring us full enlightenment. When we ask truly, we receive completely.

What does forgiveness do? It is not visions we see, but thoughts we have. It doesn't alter what mind is, but changes what mind thinks.

Our false thoughts can not be taken from us. They must be given up, turned over, released to a deeper Wisdom. Our role is simply to decide, if we want to keep feeling the same and when we don't, there begins an inner shift.

Forgiving yourself

We have a pile of unpaid bills and feel anxious. We get up in the middle of the night, worrying if we are going to put food on the table. We just don't see how to make ends meet. This has been going on our whole life. What kind of loser are we, that we struggle so much? When are we going to get a break?

We sit on our couch, in the dark. It is cold but quiet. Our family is asleep and they are safe. We feel powerless but begin to wonder if there is anything we can do in this situation.

We wrap a warm blanket around our shoulders, as ideas come to us. We know life has been a struggle, but things have always seemed to work out. There is not much we can do this very moment, but opportunities have come before. Perhaps they will come again and soon.

We really don't know what the future holds. Why are we so sure it will be more failure? Life has a funny way of surprising us, when least expected.

Suddenly, we feel a sense of hope. It is possible things will get better. But what has to change? Maybe it is me. Maybe I have to allow for more abundance in my life and not focus on what I don't have and appreciate more what I do. I have been blessed in many ways.

We go back to bed, still with bills on the table, but not so afraid and over time, one by one, they get paid.

In our life, we have many more such nights. That little glimmer of hope though, stays with us. We worry over finances, but it's a bit different. We don't feel so alone and helpless. Something is there we cannot see. We called and It answered.

I had an argument with a colleague at work today and they ended up getting terminated. I am wracked with guilt, its all my fault. I feel so badly, they have a family to support. I should have handled it differently.

Secretly though, I wonder if I wanted them fired. I never liked them. They always treated me so condescendingly. Was this my way of getting revenge? I am kind of glad they got canned. But still, they have kids.

I must be an awful person. I thought I was better than this. What if they can't get another job?

I am cooking dinner and keep thinking about the day's events. I see myself trying to blame them for what happened. But that just makes it worse. How I could possibly feel better? Somehow, I need to find forgiveness. But, they probably hate me. I cannot look to them for mercy.

Then, a sudden idea comes to me. I don't know what anything means. I assume getting fired is a terrible situation. We all need money. Though, their spouse works and they will probably collect unemployment. Still, I say to myself, that's no excuse. I am sure they don't think this is a good thing.

I sense a question. Isn't it arrogant to consider them weak and a unable to deal with their circumstances?

They had every opportunity to correct the situation. We all create our own reality. No one is ever powerless. They were unhappy at their job but couldn't quit. It might be they wanted to get fired. Who knows? Things happen for a reason.

I am not responsible for what other people do. I don't control the Universe. I don't decide their fate in life. For a moment, I feel a sense of relief.

I am guilty though, I protest. People at work will hate me. I will always be the one who got their friend fired.

Another thought enters my mind. What other people think of me doesn't really matter. They are responsible for their perceptions and I for mine. If they choose to see me in a negative light, they feel the effects of that decision. It only matters what I think of myself.

Oh come on, I argue. That is justifying my actions. Surely there must be some negative consequence. We can just get away with our behavior. Where is the justice? We must be punished somehow to make amends.

I go back and forth with myself the rest of the evening, with no resolution, tossing and turning all night. The next day, driving to work, I feel apprehensive, expecting some fallout and then nothing really happens. Some ignored me and a few just shrugged their shoulders. But there was no mob seeking vengeance.

I realized, I alone was my tormenter. It was true, others might have thought poorly of me. But was my self-condemnation just? Was I really doing the right thing by torturing myself? Was my guilt valid? I knew then, I lacked understanding and the forgiveness I needed, was my own.

Forgiving ourself may seem easy, but it is not. We are, oftentimes, our harshest critic and own worst enemy. We think, somehow, we are being a good and loving person, by holding our feet to the fire; condemning ourselves for mistakes we have made or missteps we have taken.

We imagine, in berating ourself, we appease the gods and gain their favor it makes us more humble and so, Life might treat us more favorably.

If we forgive ourselves, for what others deem bad behavior, or evil actions, then we are considered to be psychopathic, without a conscience. But true correction and atonement for our sins, is not found in being punished. It is really in the redemption of our perceptions.

Forgiving others

We are driving through the middle of an intersection, when suddenly, we're hit on the passenger side of our car. For a moment, we are in shock. It happens so quickly we don't have time to react. But after the car comes to a stop, we are shaken but not hurt. We get out to look at the damage.

It is obvious, the accident was caused by the other driver going through a red light. It was then, our confusion turned to anger.

We are outraged by their failure to obey the law and jeopardizing our life. We turn to confront them and start yelling. We just want to beat them senseless. Then we see an elderly woman sitting behind the wheel, in a daze, her airbag deployed.

Initially, we are taken aback. But then our anger returns. She shouldn't be driving, if she doesn't know to stop at a red light.

The police arrive and we are brought to the side of the road, to explain what happened. They agree, it is clearly her fault. Hours later, we are still shaken, being driven home.

The next day we wake up to a stiff neck and pain down our back. We end up going to a Chiropractor for the next several weeks; not a pleasant experience. We continue to be upset.

Our anger gets worse, when we find out we have to pay our deductible and can't sue anyone, because of a clause in our insurance. Our car is stuck in a repair shop and will forever be listed as being in an accident, reducing its value.

The old lady didn't even get a ticket. It's outrageous. Just thinking about it brings our blood to a boil. How is any of this fair? What did we do to deserve this? Every time we think about it, we just get upset.

After months of being annoyed, with no resolution, we decide we're not happy. So what can we do? Of course, we don't imagine anything will make us feel better, because we can't change events. But, we open the door to the possibility and turn it over to Inner Being.

We are adamant though, what she did was wrong. We won't change our mind about that. But, in recalling the day's events, we remember a curious impulse.

On our way home from an appointment, we passed by a fast food restaurant. We felt hungry and had the idea to get a few hamburgers for lunch. But, we were in a rush and questioned, "Why spend the money when we can eat for free?"

Another thought then crossed our mind, "Why continue to suffer just to save a few dollars?

Instead of stopping though, we chose to continue driving and it was not long after that the accident happened. Looking back, we now regret our decision. If we did, we would not have been in that intersection at that specific moment.

It wasn't our fault at all. But, in a way, we decided not to listen to our gut, literally. Now we weren't so sure it was all her doing and we didn't have some part to play in that drama.

We remembered then, reading somewhere, there are no accidents in life. Everything happens for a reason. But why would we do that to ourself? That doesn't make sense.

For arguments sake, we thought, what intricate planning does it actually take for two people to be in the exact same location at precisely the same time. Did the Universe conspire against us?

We start to feel guilty, questioning if this was our karma? But then we think, if she didn't hit our car, it would have been someone else. Perhaps, someone with a child in the backseat. Maybe, by hitting us it prevented something worse.

We never find out why the woman ran the red light. We can only imagine it was from her age and driving longer then she should have been on the road. Was she too stubborn to listen to her family and continued? Would she stop now? We hoped so.

We stopped being so angry, but not because we pardoned her actions. We just didn't know anymore that she was totally wrong.

We forgive others not for their benefit, but our own. Forgiveness is more than letting go of judgment. It is transcending normal awareness. It reaches to another level where we see life with greater perspective.

There is more going on we actively know, how then can we be so sure our anger is righteous?

Forgiveness is undoing. It is letting go of the surety we know what things mean, when their meaning brings suffering. The Truth cannot cause unhappiness because of what it is and where it comes from.

Whenever we are unhappy, even to the slightest degree, that is when we must forgive whatever we find upsetting. Especially, when we think we are right, because if we are unhappy then we are wrong.

Forgiveness is not something we do ourself. We cannot transcend anything alone. If we made the problem, how can we give the solution? It is the same process of dealing with all illusions - turning within to a Higher Wisdom and asking for greater Understanding.

Forgiveness is having perception corrected, by allowing the Greater Self, to undo all errors in thinking and replace our false thoughts with those that reflect what is true.

What we forgive,
no longer has power over us.

In unforgiveness, we are prisoners of what remains outside our influence. But in releasing what disturbs our peace, we are no longer bound, but free.

The forgiveness of fear

We think fear must be overcome in the world, before it can be released by the mind. But this is a defense against its correction. If it is to be overcome at all, it must be at its source. Conditions do not cause trepidation, beliefs do. It is our perceptions then, that need to change.

But, if we feel powerless in fear, how is it possible we have power over fear? Regardless of what the ego says, it is the power of the Mind that creates it and it is with the same power it is undone. Like all false thoughts, we must learn to forgive fear, to let it go.

If fear is the defeat of our will, then its opposite must be what fulfills it and that is only Love.

Fear and Love are mutually exclusive, where one is the other cannot be. That is why the Bible says, "perfect Love casts out fear." When we are apprehensive, we are perceiving lovelessly. When we look with love, nothing we see can cause us to be afraid.

Forgiveness is Love and
Love is the end of fear.

With Love, we transcend fear and leave it behind, like an threadbare blanket, we once thought gave us warmth, but really, kept us in rags.

Whenever we are afraid then, it is because we have chosen to see the world, without love.

If perception is based on belief, then loveless perception means, we have decided what we see is unlovable, not worthy of being loved or, doesn't love us.

Love is based on Oneness and oneness implies sameness and equality. We judge against, what we consider to be unlike ourself and shares not our will. The root of all unloving perception is the belief in separation.

Separation creates fear.

We are walking down the street and confronted by a stranger, wielding a bat and demanding money. Our conditioned reaction is going to be fear. They are not seeing us with love, but as their victim, a target to destroy.

We can respond in many ways - with anger, with panic, even compassion for their desperation and depending on the meaning that determines our experience.

When we think someone is attacking us, we also believe they do not share the same intention. They want what we have and if we don't want to give it to them, we interpret their demand as a threat.

It is not the possibility of being hit with a bat, though, that causes fear. It is the idea we are separate and opposed to each other. We could just as easily stand unafraid, if we had no attachment to money or even our own safety, for fear is losing something we value.

Jesus would not be afraid but bless their attacker, knowing of their great need. Buddha would be at peace and give whatever money he had, being unattached to such material possessions neither would judge the situation from a separate point of view, for both live in the Truth.

Separation creates fear and its undoing is found in the recognition of Oneness. But we cannot see that greater reality, while we continue to peer through the lens of ego individuality.

It is inconceivable, to perceive opposition and think of joining. It is also not possible, to look through the eyes of ego and not be afraid, for from that vantage point, everything stands against us.

Being fearful is inherent to what ego is and fear can never be overcome with its help.

**The letting go of fear,
is also a reliquinshing of egoness.**

If Oneness is reality, separation is illusion and with all illusions, while we want them to be true, we cannot let them go. But, there is another aspect of fear, that lies hidden in the background, unnoticed but very active.

Fear comes from attack but, not the attack itself. It is the belief we cannot defend ourselves, that ever causes us to be afraid of anything.

If a young child started approached us with a bat and wanted money, would be terrified? Or perhaps amused? We might laugh instead of run.

Fear is the belief in powerlessness.

Powerlessness is the foundation on which all fear is built. It comes from identifying ourselves with what has little influence being a body limits our power over outside events.

Bodies cannot join, only minds can. Forgiving fear is coming to the deeper recognition we are not just a body, but a Mind. We are beings of Energy. But that requires the willingness to see ourselves differently.

When we think we are just a physical being, separate and alone, what can we feel but a sense of weakness and vulnerability? When walking down the street, how can we not think we could be attacked at any moment. In dwelling on differences, is Oneness conceivable?

To truly be free of fear, we must connect with our Inner Being and learn of our True Nature. Where is it then, in the calm recognition of our inherent power and strength?

The end of fear,

is in the awareness of Eternal Being.

The forgiveness of guilt

Guilt is condemnation for doing something wrong and calls for atonement. In our world, atoning means paying a price. That is why all guilt leads to fear.

We believe we cannot make things right, without a penalty. Justice, in our eyes, does not ask for forgiveness, but punishment.

Can you imagine the outrage, if a murderer was released from prison, without serving any time? Or, a rapist allowed to go free, not even a slap on the wrist?

We believe, without consequences, criminals would run rampant and they probably would. Soft-on-crime approaches are shown to increase crime, not lessen it. So we create a system that seeks to maintain law and order, unless civilization devolve into chaos.

The purpose of issuing traffic tickets is, to inflict pain on people who break the law, with a monetary consequence. In our society, money supports life. Isn't then, our life taken from us, in some small measure, as restitution?

If wrong doing does not exact a price, we imagine life itself would be destroyed. So, we must conquer the evil doer instead.

Guilt demands death.

Wrong decisions and actions, do call for correction, not because the Universe would suffer. But, that we suffer over our mistakes and that is not the Will of Love. Being punished for our sins, however, does not lead to redemption. It only reinforces false thinking, by making it real.

Punishing guilt,
only reinforces guilt.

Guilt is predicated on the belief we have the power to change someone's nature to undo the Will of the Universe. Would we feel guilty over attacking someone or something, if it had no effect on them? No. What has no results does not exist, for only what is real can affect change.

All guilt is a delusion.

Guilt is a delusional idea we can change the nature of Creation. We do have the ability to break humanity's rules, but we cannot go against the Laws of Truth.

But, we believe we can and experience the trauma of that belief in a powerful way. So, we assume it must be true. Guilt seems all encompassing, because it creates fear, which can be overwhelming, as it is threat to our life.

As fear is the belief in powerlessness, guilt is the belief in unworthiness.

Guilt is the belief in unworthiness.

Worthiness comes from doing and giving things of value, for we are what we extend. In life, what has the greatest meaning but what fulfills Will and that is Love. When we feel guilty, we are declaring ourselves to be an unworthy person, having acted lovelessly. Through our negative judgments, we have tried to give another what has no benefit and received that for ourself.

To forgive guilt is its undoing, because it is replacing love with anger or hate and giving only what is good.

When we forgive another we give them the love they have denied themselves. When we forgive ourself, we let go our illusions about who and what we are and remember our True Self.

Forgiveness shows us, guilt is not real, because no matter what we do, we cannot change the purity of our Inner Beingness, nor the purity of another.

But there is one obstacle to overcome and this is our resistance to letting guilt go.

It seems illogical to say, we willingly hold on to what causes us pain. But nevertheless, when we do not seek healing through forgiveness, it is because we choose not to.

Why would we want to suffer with guilt, if we can be free of it?

We are deceived into believing guilt is some form of Love. The ego, argues, if we do something wrong and feel no remorse, we must be a heartless person. Guilt demonstrates, deep down, we are loving and that is what we want to hear. So really, it is a good thing and does not need to be forgiven.

But, underneath, there is a hidden motivation for continuing such feelings. In secret, the ego rejoices every time we feel guilty, because that is proof we have fractured the will of Oneness and separated ourselves from Eternal Being.

For us, that is enough to establish the ego's reality in our minds. If guilt and fear are Love, then Love cannot be Itself and what more perfect way to destroy what It is and keep a little piece for ourself.

Love was given to us. We did not create it and do not determine its Nature. But ego is about having the power to make what it wants be Truth and fear and guilt are its attempts to control reality.

If both are founded in separation, how can they be loving, when Love is the Unity in all things?

Love would never say we are guilty of anything, because we cannot be apart from our Source and sin. Nothing exists that can transgress against the Lord of Heaven and no power is greater than All That Is.

When we believe otherwise, we are living in ignorance and lack true understanding. Should we be punished for our mistakes, or enlightened? Should we be condemned to damnation or returned to right thinking and redeemed?

Forgiveness, not condemnation, is always the true response to the call of guilt.

The forgiveness of anger

When we are angry, we have perceived something as threatening and are afraid. But, instead of letting fear overtake us, we attempt to get rid of it by projecting it outward.

Anger feels good because we think we are protecting ourselves. We see it as a power, used to overcome an enemy. The greater the threat, the angrier we are.

Whoever went into battle singing happy songs? Generals embolden their armies through rage. When in combat, anger serves a purpose. It is a shield, a suit of armor. It ignites the passion to kill.

In living life though, we are not at war with the world and being angry works against us. It shatters our peace of mind and doesn't achieve our ultimate goal.

It is not just about the body. It is also the mind and the thoughts it holds.

Anger is an ego protection; a method to try and change someone's mind, by making them feel fearful or guilty. We rationalize our righteous indignation, as being a justified reaction to first being attacked ourself.

We get angry, whenever something opposes what we believe, because life is sharing and what does not share our will we perceive as against us. Even the slightest annoyance comes from some misperception of being opposed and defeated.

We must learn to forgive anger though, not that it is necessarily wrong. Rather, because it is based on what is false. The real issue is not anger, but the fear that causes it.

We must ask ourselves, "Why are we so mad?"

The answer will always be, because we are afraid.

But, what are we afraid of?

Something we don't want -- a defeat of our Will, some form of death we will encounter if we don't respond forcefully.

Forgiveness though, would show us, the real goal of anger is Love, for we seek to get what increases, not lessens our Will. But, how can we get others to support us, when we attack them? It is not possible.

When we give up being angry, we realize, our True Will cannot be defeated being the One Will we all share. When we give Love, we receive Love. But it must be given in a way that is understood.

Anger can never bring peace, nor the awareness of that which Unites us All. Why then use it, when it doesn't serve our purposes?

The forgiveness of hate

Hate is just another aspect of anger. It is the opposite of Love, because it is founded on fear. It does not exist unto itself, but is a response to being afraid.

We hate what we fear.

Hatred, being part of anger, appears destructive. But in truth, its basis is powerlessness. How then, can it be truly powerful?

Hate groups are about division. Their founding principle is strife. Those who deride others together, are still lost in the illusion of separation and sow discord, believing it is unity.

But, we cannot band together under the banner of hate, thinking it is the call to Oneness. We cannot despise anyone and love ourself.

Fundamentally, it is a lack of self-love that is projected onto who we see as different; a feeble attempt to see others as unworthy, instead of ourselves.

In darkness, it is evil. In the light of forgiveness, hate is a question being asked, "Why am I not loved?" For they are the ones that feel undervalued.

When we hate another, we first hate ourself.

Forgiving hatred in our self, undoes its source, which is unworthiness. When self-destructiveness is replaced in the mind, with self-preservation and we recognize our own self value, hate has no place left to dwell.

We cannot oppose those who oppose us and expect to find peace or happiness. Forgiving hatred in another, is letting go of the illusion they have the power to affect our Inner Being.

It doesn't matter what they think or do, how vicious they are and evil their shouts. Their hate can touch us not and will but swallow them, to drown in their own misery.

When we love our enemies and bless who would persecute us, what we see are not those who stand opposed, but those who stand against themselves. For the light is within them, though they refuse to recognize it is there. But, in our compassion, we can acknowledge it for each other and see it is everywhere.

The forgiveness of death

Anything that disturbs our peace of mind, brings a twinge of fear, the pain of guilt, a flash of anger, or a burning hatred comes from death.

Death is the heart of darkness; the master of all illusions. It is the dark Sire of despair and the evil Bearer of every sorrow. It comes in a loud wailing, or a soft whisper of destruction we listen to, like a wise counselor, a faithful friend.

We question not its intentions, deceived that it speaks the Truth and in seeing through the body's eyes it does. So, we uphold its reality and carry the heavy burden of its cross our entire lifetime, only to make our journeys more wearisome and finally, futile.

But strangely, there is part of us that rebels against the idea, and refuses to give up, as though there is something more to life we see or know. It is like an echo of faint melody, barely heard, yet reminding us of another home we once had; a happier place of love and unending joy.

In every hope we have, in all of our searching for happiness and peace, when we rise in the morning with a smile, embrace our children and believe in their future, we are seeking the end of death.

How is death overcome?

There is no darkness so impenetrable the Light cannot dispel it. If forgiveness brings the Light of Understanding, then by forgiving death, it is transcended.

Forgiveness in a traditional sense, is letting go of condemnation. It is saying what is done is done, but we choose not to punish it, for whatever reason.

But physical death cannot be undone, nor pardoned for what it does. Death would be the final and complete defeat of our will. How then can it ever be accepted?

If death is true, it is forever, unforgivable. But Love says it can be and so, we must be able to know death is not real.

Why was the life of Jesus, so impactful on human history? Over two centuries later, his words still resonant in the hearts of many.

He preached about kindness and love, but that is not the reason. Many others who spoke the same words, have long been forgotten. It was what he demonstrated to be true, that changed the world.

Through his miracles he proved the power of the mind over the body and the spirit over the flesh. In his resurrection from the cross, he defeated death, the center of all sorrow in life.

Jesus proved death is not real and if we follow him, we are led to eternal life.

Buddha in his enlightenment, remembered his eternal nature and taught the world the body was not the beginning of life and death was not its ending. The spirit of a person, their Energy, cannot be destroyed, but only passes to a higher state of Being.

He demonstrated, it was possible to gain that understanding through right practice and in Clarity, its falsity is revealed.

There is no death.

There are many spiritual paths in world and they all lead to the same place, the same conclusion. Life is Eternal and what lives has lived before and will live after this form comes to an end. But, to find inner peace in human existence, we must come to know that now.

It cannot be, we have to die to prove we survive dying. There is a certainty we must find in our day to day life, that reveals to us the Greater Reality of Unending Existence.

In a world that is ruled by perception and not knowledge, where beliefs determine what we see, it is in our minds, where death is laid to rest in peace.

See not death anywhere
and you will see Life everywhere.

Forgiving the demise of the body is perhaps the last thing we do. It takes profound insight, to see the end of the physical form as a happy return to our original state.

To achieve this understanding, we must learn to forgive all the smaller, myriad ways this idea manifests itself in our life. It is by learning to overcome these little deaths, we eventually come to see beyond its final expression.

You know you believe death is real, whenever you feel:

A situation is hopeless.

There is a lack that cannot be filled.

I can achieve my goals by attacking another.

I am a failure and will never be a success.

I have done something wrong and will be punished for it.

Life is meaningless.

I am powerless. I am worthless. I have nothing. I am nothing.

Whenever we feel a darkness closing in on us, are afraid or depressed, anything that brings unhappiness, it is in that moment we must turn within and Call for Love to save us.

Releasing death is a return to Life, to faith and hope. Love will always transcend the belief in mortality, for Love comes from the Eternal.

Love is the Light and when you call, It always answers and banishes the darkness.

The forgiveness of our self

It has been said and often, we choose what we want to be true and in all of our negative experience, we are deciding to believe the body is more real than the mind.

Inevitably, we are led to question -Why would we want to have faith in our own powerlessness and destruction? The answer we have seen, is it supports the ego's existence that we are a separate being apart from each other and All That Is.

There is another question though, we need to ask and it is, what is the ego and why do we want it?

The ego is the self-perception, we are what we are not. It is an idea conceived in timelessness, that what has no end can end, Truth can be given to illusion, love can turn on itself and chaos can replace sanity.

It is a decision for choices that do not exist and what is immortal can be brought to mortality and die.

It would seem then, we have turned against the Universe and attacked it, wanting to take our little life and fence it off from the rest of Creation.

In sad consequence, when we exist alone, we fear bringing down the wrath of god and shudder in terror, waiting to be struck down for our vile sins.

We believe in our own guilt.

The ego would have us believe, what we think about ourself is always true, otherwise, why would think it? But unless it brings us peace, it is must be false.

It is the separate self that is the cause of our every trepidation and sorrow. It is only this self, grasping onto the solidity of form, that believes in death and trembles in the night. We know we think this is what we are, whenever we do not have a sense of belonging, of value and some connection with the world.

This is living our own life apart from others, where no joining is possible and only our survival matters. But, such an existence has no meaning and no purpose. How can it ever make us happy?

The ego though, is just an idea in our minds, not a being of its own. We are still as we were created to be and egoness can be transcended in the remembrance of Oneness and the sharing of Life.

We are not alone.

We do not exist apart.

All Life is One.

When we forgive ourselves for wanting to be an independent being, we recognize, nothing we ever pursued on its behalf brought us happiness. Perhaps we thought it did, because getting gave a sense of satisfaction. But it was not the deep sense of fulfillment that gives life meaning.

What the ego wants is not our Will.

This is the only thing we ever learn.

We realize what Self is, by understanding our Will. In all situations where we must make a choice, or decide on a course of action, we must ask, "What is my True Will here?" That answer reveals what we are.

In forgiveness we discover, the only thing we ever wanted was Love.

We sought to leave our place in Heaven, to be born in a world of pain and suffering. It is a journey that may seem to have no reason.

Though, in the end, everything serves the Greater Good.

Forgiveness is the light we bring into the darkness of illusions and returns our confused minds to Clarity.

Separation is not an idea that is born in the world. It is the idea that gave birth to the world. So, It is here we must forgive what needs no forgiveness in Truth.

Who forgives the ego? We do not do it alone. It is the whole of our Self and each part plays a role. We who see the body and the mind that thinks it real, turns within to our greater Self who reaches back to its Greatest Self and is reminded of its Eternal Oneness with All That Is. As it was received, so it is given us to manifest and we learn what we are, by what we extend.

We who would forget, come to find Peace and in our renewed awareness is Heaven restored, to those who could never lose it.

In a place of forgetting,
we come to remember.
This is the purpose of the world.

A Seventh Truth

The World

In a moment, so long ago, before memory was, the Universe exploded into being; power beyond comprehension released in every direction. Swirling energy expanded and coalesced. Gravity pulled matter together, forming galaxies of suns and planets. Billions and billions of years passed.

Life emerged in the deepest oceans, climbed out and crawled across the landscape of dry land. In time, reaching up to stand and then walking through the forests and over the mountains, sentient beings scattered across the Earth.

Hunters and gatherers become farmers, coming together in groups and clans. Encampments became towns and cities became nations, as civilizations rose up and grew on every continent.

Today, we have a history. We dig up bones of beasts long forgotten, looking to solve the mystery of how we got here. In the darkness, we peer into the night sky with our science, hoping to answer the question – why? We want to discover the origins of our life, so we can know its meaning and purpose.

But Truth is not in the dirt and the rocks or the clouds of dust and debris that remain from that beginning moment. It cannot be found in some distant past, nor is it out there in the hushed silence of space.

What is the world and who are we in it? This is a question many have asked and much has been given in response.

Science can tell us about the mechanics of the Universe. But It doesn't know the Why and without understanding its purpose, we cannot know its meaning.

What has reality can be known and understood. Since we exist and the world exists, there must be something behind it all, we can understand.

The physical Universe as it appears to us, has no apparent motivation. It's not growing to anything greater, just expanding outward. There's no evidence we can see that shows a purposeful intent. It just seemed to happen. Out of nowhere it came into being.

Stories of creation abound, but none really fit the reality of physics, or the evolution of life on Earth. Many researchers have tried to discover, the quantum meaning behind the galaxies. Does the number Pi somehow prove God exists? Are we looking for contact with other intelligent Life, so they can explain how it all arose? They believe, if they can just understand what caused the Big Bang, they will finally solve the equation.

What is the world?

There is the planet Earth – the spinning blue globe, orbiting the sun, its axis tilting back and forth, causing the seasons. There is the wind and ocean currents. There are the valleys and the mountains, the lakes and the rivers. There is an incredible array of life; nature in all its wonder.

Then, there is the world. There are countries with borders, and roads to somewhere. There are governments that people rule and governments that rule the people. There are clocks and time zones. There are books and movies, phones and computers; civilization in all its glory.

The World and the Earth are not the same. The Earth is the stage on which the play is performed, the screen on which the movie is shown. It is the form, the body, the physical.

The world is the drama acted out, the adventure told, the story that is written. It is the content, the mind, the non-physical.

The Earth is a place in the Universe.
The world is an idea in our minds.

Our entire civilization is the outward appearance of inner thought. It is the manifestation of what we have come to believe society should be. We are not fated to a certain destiny and bound by laws we cannot change. As it was created in the past, we create it today - out of our imagination.

Most of what we do every day, is related to the realities of the body. We eat, we breathe, we relieve ourselves, we sleep and reproduce. We are born, we live and then die. These are the foundations of physical existence. Over millions of years, they have not changed and never will.

Society is our response to these basic functions; it is the mechanism we have devised, to fulfill those needs. The global economy, nations and countries, money, credit scores, banks, fashion, art, culture, music and everything else are joint decisions humanity has made.

There are certain rules we agree on. Though, these are not rules of the road, or rules of state. They are more fundamental. These beliefs are the basis of daily life.

The World is an Agreement, we all share.

We accept the idea of time and space even though, there is no absolute dimension or duration. A year of time has no meaning. The length of a galaxy is an arbitrary number. It is all relative to point of view. These are conventions decided on, to help us understand our world. They are not definitive aspects of the Universe, but structures in which to order events.

The most central belief we share, upon which the others rest, is that we are physical beings living our own life. We have agreed to accept perception as the Truth and see ourselves, not as a collective Energy, but as separate individuals, struggling against one another to survive.

The world operates on this root assumption, so deeply buried in our psyches and history, it is not seen as a belief at all. It is a very fact of reality and to question it, is to question our own sanity. Yet, there is evidence and experience, something more exists.

The truly know ourselves and ultimately, the entire Universe we have to understand that everything is one thing, manifesting as two.

There is first energy and its appearance as matter. There is the non-physical preceding the physical; the mind superseding its counterpart - the body.

When we fail to understand the true nature of things, we become trapped in false perceptions and from there we make choices and decisions not reflective of the truth. We don't live fulfilled lives, because we are operating with half understanding, for fulfillment only comes from wholeness.

When we see ourselves as mere mortals, we limit our identity to what perception shows. But, when we understand, foremost, we are energy and mind, our sense of self stretches outward and is no longer bound by physical boundaries. From this greater perspective then, the world we can create would be far more expansive than it is now.

It is an inherent aspect of Life to seek for continuation. But it is only through growth and expansion that life continues.

In our society, there are many theories about the next step in human evolution. Some think it is accessing more brain function, based on the false idea we only use 10%. But this is misleading. Our body already functions at the highest level. Of itself, there is nothing more the brain can do to advance humanity. There is no pill we can take that will expand our vision and knowledge. More brain power is meaningless, because it is the Mind that thinks, not the brain.

There is a false optimism, found in many popular movies and best-selling books, that one day, humankind will be visited by alien beings. If they don't destroy us, they might save us with their advanced knowledge and all of our questions will finally be answered. Or, that we ourselves will leave the confines of the Earth and venture out into space, exploring worlds unknown.

Human imagination is great, but physical reality has its limits and we cannot travel in space for thousands of years to reach the nearest star cluster. And who can say what we would find, when getting there?

It's unrealistic at best and tragic at worst, to place our faith for a happier future on fantasies that will never come true. While we believe the impossible is possible, we can never discover the real possibilities for a better world.

The world has to evolve, if it is to survive. But what it will become is not predetermined. The choices we make today, will decide what it is tomorrow.

Who would say we are all living our dreams? Is the world at large fulfilling its potential, where everyone has the opportunity to live their best life? There is nothing keeping humanity from being at peace with itself, in harmony with the planet; a place of happiness and celebration of life. There is great beauty here and Love, it is painful so many struggle, when the Truth can set them free.

When we talk about changing the world, we are not talking about solving problems. We are not going to fix everything that is considered wrong – poverty, crime, abuse, murder, starvation, homelessness, oppression, genocide and an endless list of sorrows. These are not the real issue. They are the results of agreements made. If we want a better world, we have to first address Cause, before effects can be transformed.

The state of the world is determined by what we think the world must be and that is based on who we believe we are. If we are vulnerable, weak physical beings, separate and apart from each other, vying for limited resources, then the world will reflect those ideas. Can we not say, everything we deem wrong with the world arises from this belief?

If we are, instead, powerful beings of expanding Life Force manifesting that energy into physical form from within the greater Unity we share, wouldn't that belief give rise to a completely different world?

The next step in human evolution
is not a change of body,
but a change of Consciousness.

We do not change the world by changing circumstances. We change the world by changing minds about the world.

To change our consciousness, we have to change our beliefs. This is the real purpose of the world - to undo false perceptions and learn to manifest Truth instead.

The world was created to give physical form to nonphysical Content; to turn our thoughts into things. By seeing what we create, we can learn the contents of our minds and determine if they are in accord with the Truth of the Universe. It is a way for the Creative to learn what they are creating.

The world we create in darkness

We live in a sad world, a place of suffering, loss, famine and war. It is where the young know too early of disease and die as wilting blossoms in the spring; where mountains rumble and spout fire. The Earth itself trembles, felling mighty structures into dirt and dust.

Here lush fields sown long in labor are razed bare by aimless storms and flooding rivers. People are rendered helpless to shiver in the cold, as the memories and treasures of their life are washed away in the passing currents. Nature's all-encompassing hands which nourishes our existence, can also be Devastating.

The world is incomprehensible, where few have much and many have little. People lie to waste in ditches of forgotten countries or forsaken in well-known gutters starving, while others behind walls of glass, feast to gluttony nearby.

In great cities, the homeless are rejected and ignored for being too filthy, the sick wander the streets unattended, cast out and talking alone. Society can be a cruel home for many. It gives nothing to them with the greatest need and yet gives more to those with everything.

We idolize ordinary people who act as someone else, worshipping them as gods and fail to acknowledge those who stand humbly, but more worthy of honor.

We glorify illusion for being so wonderfully sentimental and abandon reality for being too real. We seek relief from life in alcohol and drug induced delusions and so think we have saved ourselves from pain. But in consequence, we lose our sanity and our soul.

We live in chaos and great confusion, where who knows what is right and what is wrong, what is good and what is bad. Our families can be the greatest abusers and our bedrooms the most fearful, unsafe places. Here, problems are accepted as an integral part of living and dysfunction is the norm. We suffer with the many vagaries of human existence and struggle daily to make ends meet somewhere in the middle. Our hearts break and even love seems to leave, abandoning us to the unfathomable emptiness of loss.

We can only grieve for our agony and that of the crying multitudes, in desperate pleas asking, "Is this the way the world is meant to be?"

We lock our windows and bolt our doors; look suspiciously upon our neighbors and walk cautiously down the street. We become startled by the slightest sudden noise and fear lurking figures hidden in the shadows. Even in the safety and comfort of our own home, we tremble as the horror of the world comes to us at the click of a button on a remote control.

We have made the disintegration of society a business, sold to us in the screaming headlines of newspapers and the sharp graphics of television. The bright smiles and tailored appearance of people recounting the day's events is deceptively sweet. How calmly we report of a young child's abduction, or the shooting of an elderly shopkeeper, so to avoid hating the messenger for the hateful message; all presented and packaged in the name of ratings.

Objectivity is justified as professionalism, but it is more a mask over lovelessness. We speak of great and heinous deeds with no emotion to keep our distance. In so doing, we disregard our humanity and the real message we receive is these sick events are due course for our crumbling society.

Who can say otherwise or show opposing evidence our country is not doomed, when we so readily report its demise? There is such a passivity among us that accepts life's decay in an agreeing nod and with a whispered sigh.

We seem fascinated with tragedy and destruction; eagerly seeking out tales of evil and perversion, honoring them with our interest. Who, when passing by a car accident, cannot help themselves, but must turn and look?

We line up to purchase what is taboo and secretly feel ashamed for having done so, yet return again for more. We cannot control ourselves and never seem to do what we believe is right, simply because we don't know how.

This is the world we live in and see every day. We are frightened because there seems to be no love here or real hope. Nothing makes sense and so, we conclude chaos is real and the ultimate end of our life and society is annihilation.

Though it is all so seemingly tragic, this world is but the reflection of what we hold to be true. It is a realm of illusion, because it is based on what is false. It is these ideas that make the world a place of suffering.

Only the physical world is real, nothing else exists.

The body is more powerful than the mind.

The body is my identity and separates me from all others.

I am powerless to control my reality.

Fear is more powerful than love.

Attack is more powerful than forgiveness.

For the Truth to be true it has to be proven – only what can be seen is true.

Death is the end of everything.

Life is ultimately meaningless.

The world we create in Light

It can be a difficult world for many, but there is also unbounding Joy. Every birth brings new hope, as Life continues and is passed on to a new generation.

The Earth has no evil intention. It is gentle in its workings and consistent in its process. It is a faithful friend, providing everything we need to flourish and grow.

Wealth will never be evenly distributed, when it comes from the efforts of those who seek to gain wealth. It is an effect of a cause, by those creating their own reality. What we reap we sow. Can a farmer who tills good soil, be blamed for a fruitful crop? There is opportunity for everyone, if they choose to find it.

Some are homeless by circumstance, others by default. But, when help is asked for, help is given. Society has evolved to give aid when aid is needed, but it must be accepted. There are those who prefer to live according to their own rules and shelter cannot be forced upon them. No one is ever powerless. Everything in life is a decision.

It is inherent to life, that what Lives will always seek to be free of pain and suffering. It is fundamental to our will that we want to be happy and at peace and will seek for that wherever we can find it.

We cannot learn what works, without also learning what doesn't. If we don't try and fail, we can never succeed. Taking the wrong way to its inevitable end, leads to greater certainty about the right path to take.

There is nothing here, that does not serve the greater good, when seen differently.

The world that forgiveness creates, is understood to be manifestation of inner thought. If we want to live in a happier, more fulfilling society we have to believe in what would make that possible founded on a different thought system that reflects Truth.

The physical world is real in our experience, but nonphysical Energy has the greater reality.

The Mind makes the body and is therefore more powerful.

The Mind can heal the body and does.

My greater Self is where my true identity lies.

I create my own reality, by the decisions I make. As I ask, I receive and nothing can come to me, I have not allowed to enter.

Fear is powerless and what is powerless has no reality. Love is Power and only Love is real.

Attack has no effects and serves no purpose.

The Truth becomes obvious when we stop believing in illusions.

Life is eternal and never ends.

Life has meaning and purpose, that is best understood in the Light of Love.

The world is always changing and evolving. What it is, must be what we make of it. If we want it to be different, then we have to be different, because we create it out of the power given us.

Can you imagine how glorious it can be, if one True Idea is given complete acceptance.

What would a world that wholly believed Love was more powerful than fear and hate, look like? More beautiful than we can imagine. Some might even call it Paradise, or Heaven.

An Eight Truth

The inherent equality of All
and the value of diversity

It is a myth, a lie, an illusion that there are separate human races. There is no white race, black race, brown race or any other colored race. There is only the one human race and its various expressions.

Human beings are the same regardless of their outward appearance. Genetics will tell you this. All people alive now, are descendants of the same ancestors. As groups migrated around the world, characteristics evolved in response to environmental conditions. But, their most basic nature remained.

There is no default shade of skin. It is a continuum of the same color. Put aside all historical perspectives for a moment and consider this:

Modern humans, most likely originated on the plains of Africa and spread outward from there. This seems sensible considering, it was warm all year round, unlike colder climates, where life struggles to survive.

If we live under the hot sun would we need to wear heavy garments? No and what happens to the skin when it is exposed to the sun day after day? As a protection, it gets darker and darker. So, isn't it reasonable to think, early humans who lived on the savannas of a tropical climate were probably dark? Then, as they migrated across the Earth, their features adapted to other physical conditions.

In northern hemispheres, over millennia, skin color would fade to absorb more sunlight, faces would change and noses could narrow from breathing colder air. On flat plateaus, eyelids might adjust to the glaring light and develop an epicanthic fold. But whatever the trait, it was a practical development, not an evolutionary advancement.

To sort out people based on certain characteristics and decide some features represent a more advanced level of being than others, is a false distinction. Crossing over mountains and rivers or oceans did not alter human nature. Even today, people living in urban cities, the remotest jungles, or islands isolated from modern civilization are still, physiologically the same.

Throughout history, many have purported the falsehood of race, to validate the evil treatment of others. In fact, it is this central illusion that is the source of much human suffering, in the past, as well as the present.

War cannot be waged on someone you see as an equal. War is justified on the belief, one group is superior to others and has a higher destiny to fulfill.

Slavery can only be imposed on those deemed less human, for who could put in bondage one seen as one's self? And who could bear the yoke of oppression, in the recognition of their inherent right to freedom?

Much of society today reflects these ideas, which we all believe in one form or another.

Racism and prejudice are based on ignorance and those who believe the doctrine of race are supporting a lie, whether they are the oppressors or the oppressed, for both give validity to the myth.

Kings and queens and the concept of royalty is an attempt to crown a select few with a quality above the rest, in hopes some can rise up from ordinary roots. But rulers can only be made greater on the throne of a mass delusion.

Celebrity and ego driven culture is a fiction. It is a made-up story by people who make up stories, but do not necessarily speak the Truth. Performers are not more special because they have an audience that applauds, even if when given golden awards.

The wealthy and privileged are not inherently more deserving of a good life than those who work day to day, or those who don't work at all.

Men and women are indeed different, because each has a unique purpose in physical life. Biologically, there are only two sexes – male and female. Neither can exist alone, for both are integral to the continuation of our species. But one is not more valuable than the other.

Yet, we live in a world where women are generally undervalued – seen to be less capable or competent. Though, how valid is this, when it is women, who in their Creative Power, carry humanity forward each time they give birth to a new generation, a new vision or a new way of life?

Men and women are equally important. This Truth does not lessen the power of men, it simply recognizes the power of women and Humanity as a whole.

What is equality?

Things are only considered equal, when they are measured or understood to be the same.

In our world, however, wherever there is a perceived difference, that difference will be weighed on the scales of value and someone will be judged to be more and someone less. It can be a skin color, ethnic background, language, sexual orientation, or a thousand other distinctions that seem to separate us out, one from another.

Some then are considered more important and have greater worth. Those with lesser worth are cast aside and disregarded. We climb to the mountain peak, on top of those below.

Our society becomes split into factions and classes, destroying any sense of wholeness we could feel and it is this fractured picture of humanity that is the cause of all society's ills.

Looking back, this pattern of division has occurred in every culture and many assume this must be part of the natural order. But, the real cause of this dynamic is more a failure of understanding what we see, then natural selection.

In seeing outward, we believe in our perception. We perceive ourselves as discrete material beings, apart from everyone else and daily life supports this interpretation.

When I am in pain, no one endures it but myself. When I am hungry, the food others eat doesn't satisfy me. If I die, the world goes on living. That we are individual entities, is beyond dispute.

Therefore, we conclude, because our life is not dependent on anyone else, our primary concern must be our own survival; what I think has no effect on you and what you do, may have no effect on me.

Further, I can escape the experience of what I do to you, because we are not related in any definitive way. There is no interconnection among bodies. So, what we do to another, for one another, or seek from each other, is all based on the condition of aloneness. This is a founding principle of our civilization. We all exist separate from each other.

Could the Nazis have killed six million Jews, if they thought Jews and Germans had a shared heritage? Could the Colonists have enslaved generations of Africans, if they saw their ancestors as equals? Could there ever be an ethnic genocide, in a country that felt a unity among its people?

Such evil and hateful deeds are only possible in a world broken apart into unconnected pieces, with no recognition of the inherent unity that binds all life together. In this state, human equality is both unrealistic and unattainable. Humanity is forever fated into warring factions, each seeking the destruction of the other.

If we are not considered to be the same, we will never be equals and there will never be peace amongst ourselves. So, what hope is there that we can ever achieve lasting harmony?

For every effect, there is a cause and every cause has effects. Our society, is really an Effect of the deeper Cause of our agreements about who we are and what life is.

We have all agreed, not in a conscious way, but in a conditioned way, we are bound by the limits of the physical self. We have decided to see only what eyes can see and nothing else.

We are so focused on bodies as the source of our identity, we cannot go beyond appearance to the Truth within. We are "body believers" – believing only what the body tells us is real. But there is more to us than just the physical. There is the greater part of our Being that is non-physical, that is mind that is energy.

Every day, from the moment we awaken, to the hour we go to sleep, we are confronted with the reality of the flesh. We eat and drink, see, smell, taste, flex our muscles and stretch our legs. There is no escaping it. We are physical beings, living in a material world and yet, there is something more to who we are. We think and feel, contemplate, enquire, imagine and dream.

There is no one on Earth who does not want to be happy. That is the very essence of life – if you are alive you will strive to Live and in that living you will reach for Joy. It is the Will of Life we all share that makes us One and in being One, we are equals, for we are the same.

It is not in the body where we are joined, for bodies compete against one another and as one gains another seems to lose. So, we think we have to fight to survive. But minds can become united in the sharing of ideas and hopes and as one gains, so does the other gain more. There is no longer need for conflict, only peace.

When we begin to see ourselves as more than what we see - when we look past the outer face to Inner Being, then and only then can we recognize our true equality. Looking deeper still, we begin to see the inherent equality of all things and come to understand:

Though we may appear different, we are the same.

But this sameness is not as we think things are the same. We are not products manufactured on an assembly line, the last piece a copy of the first.

A river is the same as a lake, but in motion. A lake is the same as the rain, but lies still. The rain is the same as the ocean, but rises up. In the falling down, they become One, even though in their journey, they are different.

If there were only oceans and no rain, how would the landscape grow? If there were no lakes, how would the rivers flow? If there were no rivers, where would the water go? If the water did not go, where would dry land be? If there was no dry land, life would just be in the sea. If there was only life in the sea, there would be no you or me.

Although elements can be identical in their nature, they may not be in their manifestation and it is this diversity that makes existence possible.

Before the beginning began, there existed an unimaginably dense solid state of heat and energy. Then, an imbalance occurred and the Universe exploded into Being. As the One energy spread outward and cooled, all the rules of reality were framed and matter was born. In great gaseous fields stars were created and planets formed.

On our world over eons, in the deep oceans, organisms developed with increasing complexity and eventually arose from the water onto land, evolving into an incredible multiplicity of species. In a breathtaking achievement, humankind attained consciousness and looked out through time to its origins, in hopes of finding the meaning and purpose of it all.

Today we still seek for these answers and what we discover, as it was in the beginning, it is still now.

This vast and unfathomable Universe only exists, because within the sameness there appeared a differentiation that set energy in motion. It allowed Life to emerge and for Life to continue emerging from Universal Energy there must be contrast, there must be diversity that allows for ongoing expansion.

Out of the Oneness of Life,

there must grow a diversity of Life,

for Life to continue living.

Life is not a static thing. It is a flow of Conscious Energy that is ever breathing out. Life would cease to exist, if it stopped growing. The world would die, if it did not evolve.

If we were all exactly the same, liked the same things, believed the same things, thought the same thoughts that would be a Oneness where individuality had no meaning. Whether each one of us existed or not would make no difference and where would expansion and growth be, if everything was always the same?

But, when there is a range of opinion, of point of view, of preference, then individuality matters a great deal and the Wholeness we are, benefits profoundly from such individuality.

It is only from the unity of Oneness,
that can we appreciate diversity
and it is only our diversity that enriches
our Oneness.

Variety, in all its forms, is essential for Life to go on living. For the human race to flourish, we must learn to celebrate our differences, in the context of our greater Unity and not use them to separate us into meaningless pieces.

Human diversity causes us to think, to question, to struggle, to be challenged, to expand our awareness beyond the limits of perception – to see what cannot be seen and know what lies before the universe was born.

A world of peace and harmony, is not a place where everybody is the same skin tone, political affiliation, sexual orientation, or religious belief. It is a home where everyone is valued, in the deep understanding, each person's difference, makes the Whole greater.

We are all One, joined not in materiality, but in the Spirit of Life Within, who revels in each unique Being as an irreplaceable part of the All That Is.

A Ninth Truth

Truths of our World

The Truth of money

Money is nothing. It is just printed paper. Today, it is even less than that; numbers on a screen or phone. It is merely an idea – a means of trading one thing for another. Of itself, it has no value or power. But in our world, money is everything. We can do little without it and it becomes the most cherished thing we desire.

Many think it is the root of all evil; the love of money is less principled then the love of humanity. If you're a spiritual person, you shouldn't strive for it, but focus more on helping others; poverty is somehow noble. But, this is not true.

There is no gain in being poor and no sin in abundance. Money is a tool that helps us live in our society. No one ever died wishing they had less wealth to pass on. But many have perished, cursing their empty pockets.

In life, the problem is not money, but its lack.
Having money only becomes an issue, when we
misunderstand its function.

Money is the means we use to get what we need to survive, to buy food, clothes, shelter, pay the electric bill and the mortgage. We use it go places, take vacations, give gifts. There is nothing we do that does not require money, at some point.

So, money seems to become the sustainer of our Life and the bringer of what we value.

Money becomes God.

For us, we see money as Almighty, more important than even God. If we were given the option of going to Worship or being given a large amount of cash, how many would be in the pews that day? Even Religions that call you to prayer, remind you not to forget your offering.

There is no escaping its vast influence. It becomes a problem, however, when we give it a function it does not have, nor could ever fulfill.

Money is no more than a vehicle of exchange. It arose because people who needed to barter a goat for some corn, didn't want to carry baskets of crops around. It was and is, a brilliant invention.

But along the way, people decided it meant something more than it was and served another purpose. Instead of being just a means, it became an ends. Money is no longer form but content.

**Money is a method of communication,
not what is communicated.**

What does money say? We think it speaks of our worth and value. It tells the world who we are and depending on how much we have, determines what that is.

Money is Power

We see power as the ability to get something we value. Wealthy people are considered influential because they can buy whatever they need or want. They can also influence others, by giving them money. The poor are seen as powerless, for the same reason.

It is always the rich and powerful, never the rich and powerless, or, the mighty poor. What could possibly be powerful about lacking abundance?

Power is being able to fulfill your will. If our will is to live as a physical being, then obviously money gives us that ability; having it is a necessary part of this world. Unless we could convince others to give us everything we needed, then we wouldn't need money at all.

But, what if we chose to value something else? What if we decided the spiritual life, or a simpler existence was important. Money would still be required, but not so much and we wouldn't feel the incessant drive to get it, the more the better.

Money is not life, unless we decide to be that which it supports. As long as we see ourselves being a body, we will pursue money. But, when we begin to recognize we are more, we give power to something else.

**Money sustains your body,
but it cannot sustain your Spirit.**

Money is Worth

Worth is having what is valuable. In our culture, the greater the amount of money we have, the more we are Worth. We assume then, worthiness relates to what possessions we own, the car we drive, and the house we live in.

Valued is what is wanted. When we have what we want, we have self-value. When our will is fulfilled we feel worthy and if it goes unfulfilled we don't.

**Worth comes from the fulfillment of Will,
unworthiness from its lack.**

Is it not obvious then, why we think material wealth brings self-worth? This view relates to being a body, for only the body is satisfied with the physical.

But, there is another aspect of ourself that possessions cannot complete and that is our Spirit. Nothing physical can ever bring the mind to completion, only the extension of its true Nature can.

We only find true self-fulfillment and so, personal worthiness, when we extend and manifest our Inner Being.

**True Self Worth comes from
serving our purpose.**

Money can buy happiness

Someone well-known once said, "I have had money and not had money and having money was better."

Who can argue with that? Life is so much easier when you have the ability to do what you want, when you want. There is no fun in not being able to pay your bills. We are not happy when debt collectors come knocking on the door. No joy has ever been found in being poor.

Happiness comes from abundance.

Happiness can only be realized in complete abundance, because any lack is void that cannot be filled and it is only in Wholeness are we at peace.

But can money buy happiness? Yes and no. It serves our first purpose, in maintaining the body. But, not our greater purpose, fulfilling our Soul.

If we were just flesh and blood, then material wealth would be the pinnacle of human existence. It doesn't get any better than being enormously rich or even well off.

The dilemma, however, is we are not just physical beings. We are nonphysical Energy as well. Our mind is not made satisfied by material gratification, but by the thoughts we think, the beliefs we hold and the emotions we feel.

We can have a vast fortune and be happy or miserable. We can have little wealth and be miserable or happy. It all depends on who and what we think we are.

The Truth of Government

Politics, by their very nature are divisive and so, not based on Truth. Yet, some form of Authority is necessary while we live in illusions about ourselves and each other.

The world has attempted many, each to its age. Today, we experiment with a few and maintain some from the past.

In the modern era, the ideals of socialism and communism have striven to express the reality of Oneness. While capitalism thrives on separation and competition.

Paradoxically however, socialism and communism have proven to be oppressive, because political power lies in the hands of a small elite, while democracy rests in the hands of the people as a whole.

Communism's greatest flaw is its ruling hierarchy; of having a few decide what is the best for the many. There is no real freedom of choice. People can be like sheep and would rather follow the crowd, then think for themselves. For many, the burden of having to create their own life is too much to bear. They would rather be told what to do.

Though, deep down, they yearn for more but are afraid. They are ruled through intimidation, not consent.

Democracies greatest strength is its freedom to decide for yourself what your life will be. Its failure lies in not granting that opportunity to everyone.

In America, we divide ourselves into political parties, Democrats, Republicans, Independents and everyone else.

Democrats are seen as more caring, because their policies would provide greater social benefits. Though, this requires bigger government. Republicans are deemed conservative and for smaller administration with a different set of values.

Democratic programs can enslave people into believing they are incapable of doing things for themselves. While advocating for less oversight can disadvantage many who struggle to live. Both have their flaws and neither adequately reflects Truth.

In many respects, political ideology is a war that creates more separation then Unity. What will unite America, or any country is not a particular belief system, but what serves the greater Good.

Politicians can be salesmen, selling a particular point of view and depending on our self-understanding we buy it or not. We all want to believe they only want what is best. They seem to have a noble purpose.

But we are left to wonder, is it for their benefit or ours? What is their real motivation?

We need to be wary of those who come speaking the language of Love, but have deceit in their hearts. They are as wolves in sheep's clothing and will devour us in their search for power.

Government should not serve an individual's quest for control and influence and yet, it does. Our whole system is designed around self-interest. But, while we live in a world of separation and competition, how can it be otherwise?

There will come a time though, when the world awakens from its long slumber and understands the True Nature of Life and the Greater Reality from which it emerges. Then, our societal structures will be vastly different.

An Enlightened Rule, one based on Truth, would look like this:

Everyone is given the equal opportunity to decide for themselves the Life they want to live and what they want to express.

For those who struggle, help is given.

You can do, be, have whatever you want, provided it does not impede on someone else's freedom for the same. Nor harm anyone else.

Every voice is heard, but only that which serves the Greater Good is listened to.

Those who break the law, must learn the benefit of the law and how it serves them, not through punishment but greater self-understanding.

The power of government will forever rest in the hands of the governed and no individual or group will have more influence than another.

Government is not and never will be, a substitute for self-responsibility. Ultimately, It is only a structure not a savior, because salvation comes from Truth and governments can not legislate Love.

The Truth of Cause and Effect

Many people invoke Karma as a curse. When we believe some-one has harmed us, we point a finger at the wrongdoer and declare, "Karma will get you."

When we see something negative happening to someone, we deem unloving, we say, "What goes around comes around."

If this were true though, isn't the bad thing they did to you, your Karma? The wheel of karma is always turning and no one is exempted from its influence.

Evil doers do evil against those receiving their Karma and in return, get it done to them later on? Who then, can be held responsible for anything they do, when they are just acting as agents of Fate? This doesn't make sense.

The Universe has no punishing intent and Karma is not a penalty for misdeeds. It simply reflects the Universal Law of Cause and Effect.

Karma is not about reprisals, but about creating our own reality. When we feel somebody has done us wrong, we have to consider our role in events.

Thoughts have consequences. What we think matters, because it affects our energy field. Our energy field is the accumulation of our emotional experience, beliefs and expectations.

In our life, events and conditions are first created in nonphysical reality and held there as mental images. When they reach a certain level of intensity, they cross over a threshold into physical manifestation and find expression.

This is turning thoughts into things, the sole purpose of the world. We learn the contents of our minds by the forms they take and see the results. In physical existence, everything, from solid objects to flights of imagination arise from the Nonphysical.

The Universe is the great arranger of circumstances, the aligner of events, the manager of all energy fields.

Creating our own reality is really a collaboration between us and Universal Being. When we maintain a particular thought system, we

219

are asking for that to be our reality and so, as we ask, we receive.

Nothing comes to us, we do not allow, whether considered positive or negative, wanted or unwanted. By thinking a certain way, we are shaping day to day life to conform to that perception.

How can we blame others or God, if it is we who establish the parameters of our experience? Where is guilt and blame, fear and anger, in the recognition we decide what happens to us?

Ultimately, everything serves our greater good, by showing us what we think and letting us determine, if we want to continue to maintain those beliefs.

Do these thoughts, which led to this experience make us happy? If not, we can change them and change our life.

The power is in our decision.

We are not a victim of the world we see, because the world we see is our creation. There can be no victims in a creative Universe, where everyone has the same ability.

Although it may seem hard to accept, nevertheless it is true. Everything we encounter is a product of our own inner Energy. If it is our thoughts that establish what we attract, then it matters what we think.

Thoughts matter.

Each thought we have, in some way, contributes to the overall tone of our Energy field. It is not one particular Vibration, which is why our experience is so varied. We all hold, both positive and negative beliefs and our life reflects that.

When we rail against someone else, condemn them, demean them, make them into an enemy of the common good, we are actually doing nothing to affect their Vibrational Countenance. Instead, we are doing everything to affect ours. We are making ourselves angry, frightened and hateful and this will manifest in our life, not theirs.

We cannot fool the Universe.

By judging others, we think we can fool the Universe into bringing them negative experiences. They are wrongdoers and deserve punishing. Though, it doesn't work this way, quite the opposite.

That is why Jesus said, "judge not lest ye be judged." He knew, what we extend outward, we attract to ourselves.

We live in an attraction based Universe, where all things are manifested according to their Nature. A negative thought can never produce a positive feeling. An unloving thought causes fear. A forgiving thought undoes illusions. Thoughts of destruction incite calamity and thoughts of Love always bring joining.

The more we think about something, the greater its influence becomes. Ideas of like quality are drawn together, producing similar thoughts and gain more power. Eventually, it is so dominant, it falls into our subconscious and becomes a belief; no longer a concept about reality, but a truth of reality.

In response to those strongly held ideas, the Universe brings us events and circumstances, we perceive as validation of those views.

Have you never had an experience where you said, "I knew this would happen." Though, that is not so much a self-fulling prophecy, as it is a result of how the Universal functions.

**Mind makes reality and
thoughts have power.**

To understand this principle of reality creation, is to harness the power of the Universe. It is only in our ignorance, are we ever limited to the life we are living.

When we are not happy with our experience, it can be changed, by allowing Universal Forces to change it for us. We do not exercise control but the power of choice.

It is not our job, nor within our capability, to make things happen. That is the work of the Eternal Self. Our role is to look at life and decide if it is meeting our expectations, fulfilling our Will. If it is, then we are living as intended. If not, however, there are things to be done and new decisions that need to be made.

In looking outward, we see conditions that do not bring us peace. It is then we begin the process of seeking something different, by undoing what has already been manifested.

This has been aptly called forgiveness, because in being forgiving, we are letting go of the ideas and judgments that have brought about those negative circumstances.

It is not possible to always associate certain thoughts with specific experiences. Sometimes it is quite obvious, but mostly the connections are obscure. Nevertheless, discovering the underlying cause is the same.

Circumstances have no inherent meaning and it is not in the form itself, we know the content. It is how we feel in those situations that reveals what we think and in turn, what we believe they mean.

In any instance, where we feel badly, it is our thoughts that are causing us upset. We are falsely thinking our will is being defeated.

In that moment, having called on forgiveness many times before and seeing a positive result, we ask to see the situation differently. Then, we let it go and another way of thinking will come to us, that feels better, brings more insight and simply makes us happier.

By allowing our thought system to be corrected, we are also altering our Vibrational Countenance and no longer attracting the same kind of experience as before. The less energy we give to negative thinking, the less effect it has. The more attention given to positive thoughts, the more quickly it manifests itself in our daily life.

Though, this is not something we do once. It must be done over and over. Every time, not sometimes, but each time we have any sense of unease, that is an opportunity to choose another way of living in the world.

The mind does not turn direction with sudden shifts. It moves slowly in small increments, step by step, one belief at time. We do not go from doubt and despair to faith and hope. If we did, how could there be any sense of stability in life.

If Consciousness swung drastically, we would seem to exist on shifting ground, with no real footing. Does this inspire happiness or fear?

Rather, we go from the surety of negative belief to the neutral ground of no longer perceiving with certainty and from there, we can leap into more positive thoughts.

The most powerful statement you can ever make in your life, when something upsets you, frightens you or makes you weep in sorrow is this:

I don't know what anything means.

Such a pronouncement tells the Universe, I want to let go of my illusions about myself and instead accept the Truth. Show me the Truth, I want to see It Now! New thoughts will come, inspired by a different perception and they will seem miraculous, for they are true miracles.

Be not afraid of negative thoughts and do not let them go unchallenged for the power to Live a happy Life is within you, but waiting your Invitation to enter.

The Truth of Specialness

Specialness is the idea, some individuals have a quality others do not possess and what is ordinary is what everyone else has.

In our society, we often deem those with a particular ability to be special. They have a talent others lack that sets them apart.

We don't know why some are more adept singers than others, or can run faster, throw a ball further, act out scripts with greater finesse. So, we assume, because they are better at doing certain things, they must be better.

They are the chosen ones, picked by the Heavens to be unique among the masses; the standouts from the crowd.

This idea is the main premise of our celebrity obsessed culture. We idolize people who become famous, seeking a moment of their time to get a signature and store it away, as a sacred icon, a family treasure. Or perhaps, a picture on a phone to prove we met them, to post online for everyone to see, hoping a little of their notoriety rubs off on us.

Throughout history, many have declared themselves to be of a royal bloodline that rules by divine right. But such nobility was often gained through murder and war, hardly crowned by God.

Today, we still pretend such human hierarchy exists, though more for tourism, then actual leadership.

Distinctiveness can also be imbued into the objects we make. Cars are fabricated with the same components and materials and yet, some are considered more valuable than others. Clothes, shoes, handbags are all crafted from common materials. But, stamp a logo on them and suddenly they become elevated and cost more. People buy luxury goods and display them, in the belief, they live a life more important than an ordinary person.

Being a special someone is most prevalent in romantic relationships, where we don't just love another, but are in love with them. We can still love others, though not in that particular way. That is reserved for the One.

For us, as a culture, we determine self-worth by how extraordinary others judge us to be. Even if no one thinks we are, still, we aspire to it. One day, we say, we'll make something of ourselves and be somebody.

But, what if we don't? Does that mean, in being nobody, we are nothing? Yes, according to how society measures a person's value.

In Truth, worth comes, not from what we have, but what we give. The feeling of worthiness is the result of extending what has value. In life, the only thing of any real significance is Love, where our Will is fulfilled and so, being bound by the desire to Live, we must seek it out and find It.

The issue we face, however, is that the ego does not know how to Love. We cannot have both Love and ego. They are mutually exclusive, having opposite goals and serving different purposes. One is real, the other illusion. One seeks union and the other division.

While we pursue an ego identity, we still seek for completion, but we must find a substitute and that is specialness.

Specialness wears a mask of a deception, that seems to offer us something we all can have. But, underneath, is based on the idea, only a few merit a Life different from others. In this perception, there is no equality or common ground. We are not Created the same. It is the opposite of Wholeness.

In Oneness all things are equally shared. There are no higher beings, nor any who lord over the rest. We all arise from the same Source.

No one is special.

For those who serve the ego, being One with All That is not paradise but torment, not living but death. The goal of specialness is to destroy Love's wholeness and make it what the ego can control instead. For Love would join all people together, but specialness would separate them out and keep them apart.

We cannot maintain we are special and believe we are part of the Greater Oneness. They are antithetical to each other.

Consider though the price we pay for such a belief. We must forsake everything that is real, to dwell in illusions, never to see the Light, never to know the Truth. We will not understand our true Nature, nor live in the surety of Eternal Being.

The world would offer us the glint of gold, but it is not a treasure worth seeking. No comfort comes from its embrace and those who think they stand above, only have more to lose, when it is their time to fall.

If the special get sick and die like everyone else, how special can they be? And while they pretended at having a greater life, did it ever bring them peace? Or were they just in denial of their ending and its grim hand could touch them not?

Ultimately, being special is a Self-betrayal and does not lead to happiness. They will forever be at war with Life, defending themselves against Eternal Being, Who only wants to join with them, in glad remembrance of the Love they share.

The Power of the Ordinary

The more ordinary you are, the closer to Truth you come, for reality is everywhere the same and what is universal, is the essence of the Universe.

The power of the Ordinary lies in the power of Oneness. Is there truly anything more powerful in life than being connected to everything else? How great is your Life when you share in the Life of All That Is? Can specialness rise to this magnitude?

When we recognize we are part of One continuous, never ending, unlimited Whole, all the Universe bends in our direction and when we ask, there is nothing that is not immediately given.

The Truth of Right and Wrong

Our idea of right and wrong established standards of conduct, we agree, is necessary for the protection of human civilization. It is believed, without rules, each person would do as they pleased, at the expense of everyone else. Of course, in this world of separate bodies with differing agendas, they probably would.

Right and wrong is a human concept, made as a compromise between the cohesion of Oneness and fragmentation of separation.

While we want to maintain our separate identities, we also recognize only chaos can ensue from such divergency. For a structure to stand, all parts must work together. Over centuries, both secular laws and religious commandments have evolved, hoping to mitigate negative behavior.

But, no matter what codes of conduct we institute, we can never have a society based on Ethics that is free of crime and misdeeds. There will always be someone doing what they want and if caught, being punished for it.

Morality, as a social construct, is founded on a fundamentally flawed principle, that as individuals, we all have a different will and there is no real underlying unity, that would make control unnecessary.

Is there any morality in Nature? No and yet, it still lives in harmony with Itself. We call it wild. But, there is more peace and order in the natural world, than in many cities and urban jungles. There must be something else then, that operates as a unifying factor we cannot see.

When a predator catches and devours its helpless prey, is that wrong? Or, is the right thing to do, to let it go to live on, while it starves to death? Nature is not humane and doesn't need to be. It operates from a deeper recognition of shared purpose, unlike the world we have made.

For us to have a more sane and balanced Society, we need to have a greater understanding of what Rightness and Wrongness are.

What is right and what is wrong?

In actions, there is nothing that is absolute. It is all relative to what we believe.

By our laws, stealing is illegal. But, if I lost my job and my kids are home starving and I have no money, is it wrong for me to go shoplifting for food?

What if a large Corporation, gives desperate people a credit card or loan but charges them an exorbitant interest rate. Even though they are making money, is taking advantage of someone the right thing to do? If I am the borrower no, if I am a shareholder yes.

Murder is a heinous crime, unless we are being attacked and then killing in self-defense is right. Or, if in that moment you are insane.

A foreign country constantly hacks into other countries business computers and steals their technology secrets. It's not correct behavior, but since your government does it as well, then that's just what we do to each other?

It is wrong to discriminate against someone because of the color of their skin. But then, how can it be right to give someone an advantage for the same reason? Is that how the scales of justice are balanced? Do two wrongs make a right?

In our everyday life, we are constantly having to decide between good and bad choices. In making our decisions, we can follow the principles of the law. But, no one adheres to our man-made rules unwaveringly.

In honesty, how many times in a day, do you not drive the speed limit? If you are late for a business appointment and will get fired if you don't arrive on time, are you going 25 mph?

You made some extra money selling beauty products to help make ends meet, are you reporting that on your taxes?

It's late at night, you are tired and need to go to bed, but you are stuck at a red light that is not changing. No one is around for miles. Are you waiting until it turns green?

You went shopping and got home to find you mistakenly didn't pay for a pair of socks. It's snowing out, do you get back in the car and drive to the mall to pay for them?

It has been said, rules are made to be broken. But, if that were true, what is the point of having them in the first place? Would it be acceptable, if someone broke into your house and stole everything? What if they decided to run a stop sign when you are passing through the intersection? Does that make you want to get in your car, not knowing what others will do?

Throughout human history, there have been many decrees that have discriminated against people, held them down, enslaved them, and gave permission for their mistreatment. They were unjust but still the Law. Should those at the time have obeyed them? Or were they justified to stand up and rebel?

Laws serve the greater good and while we are in this world we must strive to uphold them for the betterment of all. But, they are not sufficient enough to guide us in our everyday lives. They falter under the weight of perception, sometimes they work and sometimes they don't.

But, there are deeper principles we can look to, that can help us live a more peaceful, ordered life and have a happier Society.

In a very real sense, both laws and morals are a substitute for greater Understanding.

**A truly enlightened person is not guided
by laws or morals, but by Truth.**

True right and wrong can be powerful guidance, when properly understood.

Right is true. Wrong is false.
Right feels good. Wrong feels bad.

Truth is right. Illusion is wrong.

Only what is true is right and feels good.

That which is illusion is wrong and feels bad.

When making decisions then, the best course of action is determined by how it makes us feel.

The challenge, however, is discerning what we are actually experiencing. We can deceive ourselves into believing pain is pleasure and suffering is wanted.

As with everything in life, the ego has its own agenda and what is desirable to the separate self, may not be in alignment with Inner Being.

The ego is desperate to be right, because what is right is true. It will therefore, defend its position on every possible subject, whether it brings peace or not. So, there is another question we must ask ourselves, for greater clarity and that is, "Does this make me happy?"

While we can be confused about pleasure and pain, we cannot fake happiness. We are or we are not. There is no in between. Happiness is the real guiding light in our lives.

**Do only what makes you happy
and nothing that does not.**

Can you imagine what would happen, if everybody just did what made them happy and never did anything that did not?

For the practical mind, there would be chaos, running through the streets and the destruction of the society as we know it. The economy would collapse, crime would be rampant and nothing would ever get done. The world we perceive would no longer be, because it is miserable and happiness is Joy.

In its place, what we see would bring us peace, a connection to something Greater, a deeper sense of meaning and purpose. It is the worst thing a nihilist fears - more smiling faces and laughter, loud and rambunctious singing and a profound celebration of Life.

If people actually only did what felt good, there could be no poverty or lack, homelessness or addiction. Some would call it paradise and others would simply call it Home. It would be a world ruled by Love and not fear.

The truth is, when we make right choices, we are fulfilling our will, which comes not from the ego, but our Greater Self.

In the physical, when we are exclusively concerned with the body we seem to have a separate will from everyone else. So, what is best for us, may not be what is beneficial for others.

In this perception, however, doing what we think will make us happy, invariably can hurt someone else. Crime, violence and lawlessness are all about survival, not the fulfillment of the Spirit.

But, if we all sought to manifest the Will of Shared Being, would we need to control each other's actions and behaviors?

The Law of Love

Love too has its own Laws and when followed leads to unending Joy, but if denied, leads to suffering. But what is One can never be forsaken, so it must be, only in illusion we think we can attack Life.

What if we create a different world founded on Love and the same Will? Would there be law and order?

Love cannot steal as it gives All to All.

Love cannot kill, being the Source of All Life.

Love cannot deceive it is the fountain of Truth.

Love cannot attack or do harm to anyone, because it belongs to everyone equally.

Love is the recognition of Shared Being, how then can anyone be left out, when in Love we are all One.

There is no punishment in defying Eternal Being, but there is correction. When we do something wrong and feel guilty over it, Love does not demand we pay a price for redemption, or make restitution with our life. Instead, it calls for forgiving of the false and accepting of the True.

There are no separate wills that can clash and battle each other for supremacy. There is the One Will that rules the Universe and when we are in alignment with it, there is nothing we can do that is wrong. When we deny it, there is nothing we can do that is right.

Right and wrong are simply reminders of when we are being Loving or, being afraid. This is the only truthful thing we can ever do in this world:

Love and do as you Will.

The Truth of Insanity

The Truth is, in some way, at some moment on some issue, we are all insane. But, insanity is not a chaotic mind living an alternate reality. We can be quite logical and our thinking is delusional. A truer definition is:

Insanity is seeing what is not there.

If all seeing is based on belief, insanity is believing what is not true. It is insane, precisely because it does not exist in Reality, but we still see it in illusion.

Fear is insane. Guilt is insane.
Anger, Hatred and Evil are all insane.

What do we see that is not there?

In fear, we are seeing an enemy that does not exist.

In guilt, a Universe with punishing intent.

In anger, a cause without effects.

In hatred, separate lives being lived, with no connection.

In evil the power of death that can destroy life.

None of this is real in the Greater Reality and yet we believe it is. When we have thoughts that are not true, what are we then, but insane? It is essential, we realize, whenever we are not happy or at peace, our thinking is delusional. Otherwise, why would we seek for correction?

Sometimes, it is a great kindness not to see ourselves or someone else as evil, murderous or hateful, but mistaken and seeing what is not actually there.

In recognizing our thoughts are insane, we can then call upon our Inner Self, for correction and healing.

The insanity of self-destructive thoughts

We all have negative thoughts about the world and everyone else in it. We rarely question such perceptions, or consider changing them. They seem quite reasonable to us. So, it is no surprise, we also accept negative thoughts about ourselves, as part of life.

Consider this though. While we cannot control what others think about us, we can decide what we think about ourselves. Why then would we willingly have self-destructive thoughts?

If every thought comes from a belief, then we choose to believe in our own vulnerability.

When we imagine some negative condition or circumstance befalling us, we are giving energy to our own destruction and what can this be but madness. For what sane person would willingly give a murderer the weapon that would kill them?

**Insanity is wanting what
goes against our own will.**

In all negative self-beliefs, there is a disconnect between our physical, ego-centered self and our Inner Being, who knows only of our own eternal existence.

What are self-destructive thoughts?

Any thought that sees us unworthy or powerless.

Every thought that is not Loving, kind and compassionate.

All negative thinking that makes us feel fearful, guilty, angry, hateful, unloved, depressed, unwanted, limited, weak and vulnerable.

Whenever I think I cannot do what is wanted, have what is desired or be what I am meant to be.

When I feel I have nothing and am nothing.

If every thought serves a purpose, what goal does self-destruction seek? It cannot be the goal of Life, but of death and who does death serve, but the ego.

The ego does not regard itself as insane, because it does not believe it is part of the wholeness of Inner Being. From its perspective, following the Will of Oneness is quite mad, because it would lead to the undoing of its own separate existence.

It feels quite justified then, in tormenting us with Self destruction and while we listen to it, we will continue thinking such thoughts.

But, from a higher perspective, in looking back at the ego and all its works, it is clearly insane. It is part of our minds and our defeat would be its defeats and is this a goal we want to achieve?

No one would walk the path to their own death, knowing where it leads.

Let us not seek to escape from ourself,
but with ourself and for our Self.

Condemning ourselves for what we believe are transgressions against God and others, though seemingly justified by guilt, is always totally false. Is it just punishment to chop off our own hand? And who demands such payment? It is surely not the Universe Who only wants our well-being.

In forgiveness, we do not seek to comprehend insanity, because it cannot be understood. To try and understand it, is to think it can be appreciated. But appreciation is Love and insanity cannot be loved, because it is not true.

Let us be grateful then, we can be saved from such madness and return to sane perception and the Sanity of our Right Minds.

The Truth of Time

In absolute terms, Time does not exist. It is all relative to our perception.

Time, as we know it, is an invention. A second is an arbitrary term, based on how fast a timepiece moves. A minute, an hour, a day are just conventions.

In the physical world, it is a necessary structure, to order experience.

The age of a person is also a concept. To be young or old are body conditions. The mind has no age, it is Eternal Energy.

The body does not age but grows.
The mind does not grow but learns.
The spirit does not learn but awakens.

Time, like space, is an illusion; an agreement made that would seem to break timelessness into linear segments of past, present and future. But what is Eternal has always been and will always be Now.

In truth, Now is the only time there is and if we are not living fully in the present, we are not living at all, but are dead in the past or waiting to die in the future.

Living in the past

We assume, when we get up every morning, we are waking to a new day. But actually, we are seeing the past. All of our current circumstances are the result of previous thinking. How we perceive the present moment is based on beliefs accumulated over our lifetime. There is nothing we do that does not relate to some other experience. What we assume we know, has been learned and remembered. In a very real sense, we live in memory, not in actuality.

There is a practical advantage to memory. We couldn't possibly function without remembering what things are and how they work. But, there is also a limitation that implies.

When we judge a situation, or decide the meaning of a circumstance, it is always prejudiced by what has happened before. We set the boundaries on what it will be and do not allow for a different perception.

The people we meet and the conditions we face, are not really met. We encounter an image of them and so, there is no true meeting at all.

The inherent problem with how we view life is, unless our previous perception was correct, we are carrying over past mistakes and what caused us pain before, will continue to bring us suffering.

Living in the Future

To have a dream about what we want the future to be and envisioning the future we seek to create, are different. Dreams are fantasies that may or may not come true. Creating your reality, through understanding how the Universe works, is the right use of imagination.

When we seek to live in the future, to avoid the present, it does nothing to alter negative circumstances. We cannot change what we deny. It is only in acknowledging the present as it is, that we gain the ability to determine the future.

**It is only in the present,
we have power.**

Finding the present

In life, when we suffer over events gone by, we are denying ourselves the surety of our Reality. In our minds, dwelling on the past keeps us from engaging the present and it is only in the here and now that we live.

For many of us, letting go of the past is an impossible task. We use it as justification for our current perceptions. We fear, without it, we have no identity and if our minds were focused fully in the moment, the person we know would disappear. But, it is only in the Now that can we know ourselves.

We must forgive the past and forsake the future, to find the present.

The past is over and the future not yet begun. When we think about either one, though it may seem real, they are illusions and always lead to unhappiness.

We think it is joyful to look through old photos and reminisce about the good old days, but underneath, we mourn they are gone. In recalling a sorrow once endured, we are still haunted by the pain it caused.

Imagining a brighter future, only serves to reinforce how dark the present is. Neither the past nor the future can ever bring us happiness today.

We cannot change unwanted things gone by. Regret cannot reorder events and right past wrongs. What is to come does not exist in any tangible form. Dreaming of a warm spring day brings no comfort from the cold winter.

Peace is realized, by making those decisions that lead to peace and it is in the moment that is occurring, where we choose to forgive our unhappiness.

What brings suffering in life, in any form, but the unfulfillment of will, the defeat of our purpose to Live and continue Living. This comes from the perception of death and manifests as guilt and fear.

Guilt is the idea of having done something wrong in the past, we will be punished for today.

Fear is about what can happen, not what is happening. It is always in the future.

**We only suffer from the past or by the future,
never the present.**

What most people don't realize, is the deep resistance we have to just being in the Now of Experience. The ego self does not exist in the awareness of Inner Being. It is either remembered or anticipated; what it was or will be, but never as it is.

When we take our attention away from time and turn inward, we begin to feel timeless and touch the Eternal in ourselves. In timelessness there is only the Oneness of Shared Being. It is no surprise then, the separated self avoids the present at all costs, by trying to keep us ruminating over the past or worrying over the future.

Fear, guilt, anger, hatred, and all other negative experience accomplishes the ego's goal of keeping us bound to the slow turn of the wheel of hours and days. But in time, there is only death and in Eternity only Life.

Before time began,
there was You in timelessness.

When time ends,
there will be You in timelessness.

While time ticks away,
there is still You in timelessness,
waiting Your return.

The Truth of Sex, Sexuality and Gender.

Sex

We make too much of sex and too little, It is both overvalued and underrated. Sex, of itself, is nothing but a physical experience. It doesn't mean anything.

It can feel pleasurable or not, boring or exciting. It can elevate us or be degrading, create the next generation of humanity, or made to destroy. It is what we use it for, that determines what it is.

Does sex have an important role in our life? It may or may not.

If desire is of the mind and the mind is nonphysical, what does that say about the true nature of sex? The body only craves what it must have to survive. Sexual desire is not really a physical need at all.

If we are starving and offered bread or a sexual interaction, which would we choose? In eating food, our body would be satisfied; in orgasming, it is our mind. But, quickly enough, we' d feel the pains of hunger again.

What is our real need for sex? Consider what it is - the joining of two bodies in mutual sensation. It is a co-mingling of Energy in a physical form; a momentary expression of Oneness.

Sex is really an attempt at union in a world of separation. When we see our Self as a body, physical interchange can be a reminder of our deeper Nature. Or, we can recognize our Self as Energy and see no need for it. All true pleasure in life, only comes from fulfilling our Will.

Sex can become problematic, however, when we think it is something it is not. Though it may convey it, sex is not love. Yet, people falsely believe it is.

We can express love through the body, but cannot make love from bodily interaction. It is a common fallacy that leaves many in despair and looking for Love where it is not found.

When we use the body as a means,
it becomes the end of our suffering.
But, see it is as an end,
and it becomes the means of our destruction.

If we see the body as a way to attain pleasure for pleasure's sake, we can easily fall into the trap of believing it is an end in itself. In that brief moment of orgasm, it can seem ecstatic. But that quickly fades and we are again left unfulfilled.

If though, the body is used for communication, then sexual desire is about Communion. It is really minds that want to join and become One, not bodies who know only of separate existence.

Sex that is perceived correctly can lead to greater understanding. When its purpose is misunderstood, it keeps us bound to the body, all its frailty and inherent dissatisfaction.

Sexuality

Sexuality and gender are often misunderstood, because society does not understand we are two-part beings and function on different levels. We have, at once, a physical and nonphysical existence.

Throughout history heterosexuality has been considered natural and homosexuality unnatural. But this is a misperception of a basic Truth.

In biological terms, homosexuality serves no function in reproduction. When and how it came to be part of human experience will never be known. Can mankind flourish without it? Physically speaking yes. It is not essential for the propagation of our species.

If there were only two people left on the planet and both were men or women, humanity would perish. So, in this regard, same sex interchange can be perceived as an aberration, because it goes against the natural order and cannot add to human survival.

But we are not just physical beings. Energy can be expressed in many ways and forms; that homosexuality is an aspect of our world, shows it serves a purpose. Otherwise, it would not have evolved as part of society and continue to thrive. It cannot be dismissed as a mere deviation, because Nature does not make mistakes and is very practical. What is useful is kept and what is not is discarded.

When we embrace something, we bring it into the light of under-standing. When we repress it, we keep it hidden in the shadows of ignorance. While it does not contribute on the physical level, per-haps its greater role is to challenge us to question what is the True Nature of Being.

Acceptance is not saying something is right for us. It is saying something is not wrong for someone else. We do not have to agree with how others live their lives. But one part of humanity cannot decide what is best for the rest. It is surely wise not to judge what is not understood.

In truth, sexuality is just another aspect of how we express our-selves in the world. We were not created with a certain proclivity. We use it to experience life in a way that will teach us what we came to learn.

Gender

The biological truth is, there are only two genders – male and female. As it was in the beginning of human evolution, it is now and will forever be and no perceived self-identity can change that.

People who are Transgender, will never truly transition to their identified sex. No matter what surgery is undergone or the hormones taken, a man can never become a genetic woman, nor can a woman become a genetic man. Even though modified, the body will always be as it was born. That is a physical fact.

But, as Energy, we can feel ourselves as the opposite sex of our birth or even no gender at all and seek to express that in physical form. The will of the mind cannot be denied. Its power to manifest itself cannot be held back. In the Greater Reality, our basic nature as Consciousness is not male or female, straight or gay. It is behind all forms and yet, transcends all things.

In Spirit, before we are born, we agree to all the parameters of our life and the form we will inhabit. We choose our gender and our sexuality. The body we are born into is not a mistake. As we grow and develop, those decisions begin to manifest.

If we are one sex and realize our self-identity is another, or no sex at all, it is for a reason. We have decided that our Mind and our body will not be not be in alignment. In this lifetime, it is a path we have chosen to take, to learn the lessons that come from such a circumstance and its limitations.

Male and female are body characteristics that are immutable. But what is a man and a woman are concepts.

A man's man has often been described as someone rough and stalwart; not easily given to emotion. A woman's woman is caring, nurturing and compassionate, yet also strong underneath.

"Be a man" is a call to action, to take control and dominate a situation.

"Just like a woman" is used to describe a female who is flighty or weak.

So, the real questions of gender go deeper than just the form and need to be answered by the Content.

As a man, who are you really? As a woman, what is your true nature? Are you just this physical identity, or something more?

To see a person clearly, we first see their body and all its circumstances and conditions, desires, orientations. But then, we have to look beyond that, to the Being Within.

We do many things that go against human nature. We shave our face and cut our hair, live in places we shouldn't, fly without wings and swim underwater without breathing. We have even left the planet and went to the moon.

Being true to our Self, does not mean only doing what bodies can do; being only what a body can be. It is about finding harmony with Inner Being.

There are those of us, who do not live according to the expectations of society, though still yearn to be included and when rejected, feel unwanted. But does that mean we have to follow the established order just to feel we belong; that we can never be happy unless ordained worthy by the so-called mainstream? No.

When we deny who we are, we wear a costume from the closet of self-reproach and walk unsteadily in the shadows of Self-denial. Though we may blend into the crowd, the unique contours of our face blur and what seems to be a smile is really a suffered grin. Others may think we laugh, but truthfully we shriek and there is no hope for Joy in a life, unlived true to itself.

Our destiny is not to live bound by certain rules or preassigned roles. It takes great courage to stand apart in defense of our Truth. But unless we do, we can never find inner peace.

People who live an alternate lifestyle to the mainstream, are not a threat to be marginalized, but should be recognized as integral to the whole. They are more heroes than villains, because they challenge us to question and look beyond physicality to what lies within. It is a brilliant play of Energy that asks us to see what is not seen.

We must learn to forgive all things that make us uncomfortable, not because they are wrong, but because our perception of them is mistaken and false understanding keeps us imprisoned and not free.

So, while some things may not be necessary for human survival, they are essential for human expansion.

The Truth of Prejudice and Racism

Perception is naturally prejudicial. We only see what we believe. So, everyone, whether they know it or not, is biased towards their point of view. It is impossible to be objective or neutral, because we perceive the world through the lens of our thought system. We are all prejudiced.

Most commonly, however, when we call someone that, we are referring to their views on ethnicity and race.

People think racism is the idea that some races are of a higher order than others and you are racist if you consider yourself to be superior. Supposedly, those who are the lesser can't be racist. But, either position rests, on a fundamental delusion, that there are different human races.

There is no white race, black race, this race or that race. There is only the One Human race and its various expressions. But, that people are seen to be different from each other, because of certain characteristics is a prevailing belief. It is a way of seeing the world that divides people into groups, separating them out and keeping them apart.

The more accurate description of a racist, is one who believes in the reality of race. It matters, not which side you are on. It is the concept itself that rules your perception.

If you create art, you are an artist; a novel, a novelist. If you believe in God, a theist, if not an atheist. What you create you become. What you believe in defines you. If you uphold the idea of race by attesting to it, then by definition what are you?

When we call people black or white, that is a statement of opposites with no similarity or connection. It is though they have no relationship whatsoever. But, this is not the Truth.

Black people are not black and white people are not white. We all have the same skin color with varying intensities of melanin, as a response to environmental conditions over millions of years. There is no hierarchical order of human beings.

If people were not alike, we could never eat the same foods, breath the same air, suffer the same illness, have children together, donate blood or organs to each other, mourn the same, laugh the same and die the same.

What is humanity, if those of differing skin tones and facial features are not fundamentally one race? Genetic research has shown, all humans alive on the Earth now, are related to the same common ancestor. Everyone shares the DNA of a woman who lived in Africa millennia ago.

Science has proven this true. Why then, do we continue to believe otherwise?

In human perception, distinctions will always be given a meaning. This is the true problem of the world – giving false value to our differences.

Purpose defines perception

Racism serves a destructive purpose and we see what that is, by what it does.

What does racism do? It breaks us up, into disconnected pieces on different levels from each other. But, why would we choose to believe we are separated out, unless it brought us something we wanted?

If being alone is having no influence, then we must find a compromise between unity and division, that still gives us some sense of power.

Racism fulfills the ego's purpose of separation, while allowing us to think we are still part of a larger group. It would seem to give us permission to treat others with scorn and disgust, while maintaining our superiority. We think it makes us feel good about our Self.

As a superior race, we can join together in our mutual hatred of other races that seem unlike us and think of them as a lesser order. Isn't this what the holocaust was all about?

On a personal level, believing in the tenets of race makes the body more real than the Mind and consequently, the ego. Ultimately, the goal of all prejudice and racism is to affirm the body is your identity and the ego is your Self.

We don't have to be avowed racists to be affected by it. As long as we believe, physical characteristics have any meaning other than just being form, we will think it has Content.

If we are its victim, or its perpetrator, does not matter. If we don't see it in Clarity, we are upholding it, because all perception is a choice.

No one wants to be discriminated against. Yet, while we see ourselves as casualties of that battle, we are believing we can be wounded by another's actions and ideas. That only adds energy to the power of belief itself.

The way to undo racism is not to fight against it, because what we fight against only grows stronger. To overcome it, we must learn to forgive and in letting it go, recognize it was never true.

**Fight nothing that is false,
but defend everything that is true.**

There is a time for physical action, when war is at the doorstep, seeking our destruction. Then the call to arms can be heeded. But, in all else, attack is not an answer.

True forgiveness does not allow but corrects. In a world of illusion, Truth needs to be defended and made manifest.

The voices of hate and anger cannot be silenced, by avoidance or attack. Rather, it is Reason that will prevail, by revealing the insanity of hatred. When we look at someone, we first see their body and recognize we are different, acknowledging each one of us has our own life experience that has been influenced by those differences.

It could have been assumed, we are trustworthy or not to be trusted just based on our skin color; that we are lazy and stupid because of our weight; we are a good or bad person because of our appearance.

But then, we must ask ourselves, if the Energy of The Universe creates All Things, how are we not the same, when we are both born of the One Source?

If we could look at someone and see them truly, we would not see their body, but recognize their Spirit. We would not judge them by appearance, but seek to understand their Truth.

The end of bigotry, is in the acceptance of Oneness that heals the illusions of racial divides and inequalities. It is our wholeness that will save us and nothing else.

Our Soul

is not black or white,

red, yellow, brown.

It contains all colors,

It is Light.

The Truth of Sickness

Illness arises from our inner state. It can be said, sickness in all its forms, is caused by beliefs that foster thought which creates resistance to the movement of positive energy outward. Sickness is the result of the misdirected flow of energy.

Our body reflects what we think, whether we recognize our feelings or not. We could be instantly free of all disease by simply changing our mind, because nonphysical energy creates physical form. In truth, perfect faith in our inherent wellbeing would cure us completely of any adverse condition. This has been demonstrated by many miraculous healings throughout history.

But, who in this world has such conviction? No one. If we believed wholly in our own rightness, we would not have gotten sick. So, when we are ill, it is always that we harbor false ideas about who we are.

Yet, most are not directly aware of their belief system, let alone have the capacity to transform it. Healing is really a process of uncovering the hidden issues that led us into disease. Then, we can begin to choose a different understanding of life, which will lead back to wellness.

Only we can heal ourselves, because only we can change our minds. But we cannot change perceptions alone, because we believe in them. So, we need help.

It is a great misconception that to return to our natural state, we have to forgo developed healing practices. Thinking God will heal us, by forsaking modern medicine as an act of faith, is foolish at best and tragic at worst.

On the contrary, they provide us with a much-needed structure, in which to work. It is naive to believe, anyone can free themselves from negativity in one leap. It is only through the long struggle of inner recognition and practice, can we achieve a higher state of mind.

Sickness holds a gift from the Inner Self.

Negative emotions don't always create sickness and sickness is not always caused by conscious negativity.

In life, after an extended period of bad feelings and stress we can get sick. So, there is an obvious correlation between the two. But many times, an illness comes upon us seemingly for no reason and this is brought about by the Inner Self, as a teaching moment.

The sickness itself is not the gift. It is the chest, in which the treasure is found. It is the means by which we can attain a deeper Wisdom. Though, this is not understood until healing comes, for wellbeing is the Gift that Truth brings.

Sickness becomes a powerful lesson, because there is no place to hide. We cannot deny something is terribly amiss. So, we have no choice, but to confront ourselves with the question, "What's wrong with me?"

We cannot seek for the healing of the body alone and believe the mind will follow. Manipulating effects does not alter Cause. Rather, we seek to heal the body by first healing the mind and then, both are restored together.

Rarely, can we ever get to the root cause of illness. We do not consciously choose to be sick. That decision is made at another level of being. But, what we can do is be aware of our thoughts around illness and those we can change.

How does this condition make us feel about ourself? Do we feel afraid and guilty? Those are the issues we can deal with on a conscious level.

The Healing of Illness

It matters not where sickness comes from, only where it goes. In all Illness, we don't focus on the problem, but the solution. We give our attention, not to the disease but its healing.

Sickness will always bring up fear, guilt and anger. We know its cause by how it makes us feel. It becomes quite apparent what the problem is, when we begin to look within.

Who would ever say being sick is a good thing? It is always experienced in a negative way and so, it must come from negative belief.

**All sickness arises from the inner conflict
between Truth and Illusion,
between our self and our Self.**

Illness, in all its forms, speaks to the frailty of human existence and its inevitable demise. It is not about being Energy, but something physical that has capricious life. It is the declaration, I am a body, not a Mind.

Do you love being a weak and vulnerable body? Do you feel freedom within it or imprisonment? Do you revel in all its pains and discomforts? Its unending need to be fed and taken care of? Recognized or not, every time we are sick is a self-attack. It does not arise from Self Love, but from self-hatred.

Sickness is self-hatred.

It is hard to hear, but nevertheless true. In life, we get sick because we don't love ourselves enough not to. The slightest cold is a manifestation of an unhappy idea we think. The most severe illness reflects a deep seated belief about the inherent flaws of being human. The way to healing then, must be a return to Love.

How do we love ourselves when we are sick?

We don't, for Love is Life and sickness the opposite. We only Love the Truth in our Self and illness speaks to our illusions. The way to healing is in the forgiveness of our mistaken self perceptions and beliefs.

Forgiveness is true healing.

When we are sick, we must forgive ourselves for being sick. We need to be kinder and more compassionate in illness, not bitter and angry. We must look to others for care and seek out what healing the world offers. It is all part of the statement, we want to be Well again. It demonstrates we want to be Healed.

Jesus was a great Healer and he told those he healed, "Your faith has made you whole." Most would say, he was referring to God. He was, but also, he was talking about having faith in yourself. For he could not help those who thought themselves unworthy of being made whole.

Believe in your own inherent goodness, for you were created whole and forever remain so. This Truth will save you and heal all pain and suffering, because they are illusions and do not reflect the Reality of your Eternal Being.

In the end, all healing is turning away from believing in the separated self, because the ego does not love us and we do not love it. In honesty, can we say, in all our fear and guilt, anger and hatred, there is a sense of well being - the Will to Live?

Whenever we listen to the voice of separation, we hear nothing but our own demise. Yet, we continue on being deceived by false thinking and remain unwilling to accept we have been mistaken.

The ego, in all its work, doings and deceptions, but seeks our death. It does not care about us and secretly, we despise it for all its negativity. Though, we don't know how to let it go. So, we seem trapped by our own devices. But there is hope, even in this seemingly hopeless situation.

When we call to Love, we are answered and with it comes Clarity. In the light, we see, no matter the appearance, what is not loving is not Love and it is only that we ever sought. Ego then, is transcended, in the recognition we do not want its fearful offerings. Rather, we seek to be the Guiltless Self and live a Guiltless Life.

The World is a Dream

The world is a dream. We call it a dream, because it is not the Truth of our Greater Reality. Inner Being does not have a body and is not physical. But, even the dreams of the Eternal Mind have an existence.

In daily life, when we are conscious, we are aware of our environment. When we are asleep, we are still ourself but unaware of its conditions. In the same manner, with our inner life, when we are Awake, we are completely mindful of that Greater Existence. But, when we are not, we are still Who We Are, though dreaming of another self.

Dreams can be very real. Though our material form lies in bed, we are off on great adventures, being someone we are not, living another life. We can do impossible things - turn into a flower or a dog. They can be quite crazy, scary and even nightmarish. But in waking up, we remember our true Self and our real Life.

When we believe we are a separate body, limited, frail and weak, trembling in fear, with the trepidation of death always in the back of our minds, we are not living Truth. So, is that having a real life, or is it the dream of one?

When the Buddha started to wander around India, after achieving enlightenment, he encountered a group of men standing by the side of the road. They were amazed by his serene countenance and his light filled Aura.

"Are you a Deva?" they asked.

"No," He said.

"Are you a saint?"

"No."

"Are you a God?"

"No."

"Are you a human being?"

"No."

What are you then? " they asked, confused.

"I Am Awake" He answered.

What does it mean to be awake?

To be awake is to be aware. If you are human and ignorant of your Wholeness, are you no longer your Self and something else?

We can never be what we were created not to be. We are forever and always Energy, at One with All That Is. But, it is quite obvious, we are here as physical beings. Though is this all that we are?

To become Awakened is to be Enlightened; to turn on the Light in the darkened room of our mind. And in that instant, you see where you are, what you are and who you are. There are no more illusions. There is only the Truth. Your True Nature is revealed and you have Clarity and Peace. There are no longer the battles of the false self, only the Unity of the One.

We all have our moments of awakening; a sudden realization we are more than what we see; a remembering of a long forgotten song we once sang and still sing, though hear it not among the clamor and din of the world.

Some people sleep their whole lifetime, without the impulse to wake up. They enjoy the dreamworld and are trapped by it and only find release at its end.

But, there are those of Us who realize, it is all a mirage, a great charade being acted out on the stage of atoms and molecules dancing together like leaves falling from a tree, taken by the wind and swirled around, until quietly resting on the ground.

It is delightful game when we know what it is. It is only tragic when we forget.

Would you remember Who You Are? Before we were born we had a Life. After we die, we will have the same Life and in between we had not a Life but dreamt a dream.

Perhaps, this is the moment we decide we had our fill of empty promises and false hopes. We would rather begin something new, that leads to waking, of walking through fragrant scented meadows, on a soft path with those we Love.

We need but ask this simple question. "What is the purpose of the world and why am I here?"

The world was created that the Immortal could for a moment, believe that can change their true Nature, to be as they were not created. To live awhile a physical existence and then appear to die.

The world is place of choices that do not exist in the Greater Reality, but seem to exist here. We choose between the body and Spirit, the ego and Eternal Being.

The purpose of the world is to learn to awaken from the long slumbering dream of fear and guilt that keeps us bound to suffering and misery.

It is a place to come and forgive our illusions and Love ourselves again.

In the midst of all the world's forgetting, it is where we come to Remember.

It is where we can pretend to be God, but finally Understand it is not our Will to be more than what we are, to want only what has been given, to cherish what is ours.

It is here we recognize that no matter where we go, or what we do, our Eternal Source is always with Us.

A Final Truth

GOD

Is there a God, long portrayed in ancient books and stories, as set apart and watching over Creation? No. There is no throned Being with a long white beard, meting out judgment over the righteous and the sinners. There is no heavenly Deity looking down from above, deciding the fate of human beings, picking and choosing who gets what.

That is humanity's attempt to place blame for their own creations onto some mysterious Being, who never seems to show Their Face; an absentee landlord on vacation, who merely collects the rent of souls. It is the vision of the powerless, who fail to take responsibility for their role in their own Life. Yet are hoping something out there can save them from the pain and despair of mortal existence.

Throughout history, we have been searching for a God that does not exist and so, we have failed time and again to find a deep, meaningful connection amongst ourselves. The gods we believe in, have only created division and inspired many wars and much suffering.

If such a God existed, this could not be. A Creator of All things, would not choose a few and leave the rest to wander lost, only to die in the desert. Or, burn forever in the torment of a nightmarish hell. No, this is not true. We must accept that such a God does not exist, if we are ever going to realize the Truth.

Is there a God? It seems there is no direct evidence such a being exists. There is faith, but people believe in things that are not real or lies appearing as Truth. So faith alone is not enough.

When we do not believe there is a God, it is always for one simple reason, our perception does not reveal any proof there is One.

But, ask yourself if you have the courage to know what is not perceived; to forsake the small comfort that comes from believing only what you see; to be willing to open your mind to another Vision - a deeper and more profound understanding of Life.

Is there a God? No.
But is there God?
Yes! Oh Yes!
There is God and only God.

What is God?

God is the Creator of All Things. The Universe we see and the ones we don't. God is always present, everywhere, unlimited and infinite. God is All Powerful. God is the All That Is and as such, could not possibly be a physical being.

God is the Energy of the Universe,
both seen and unseen.

God is not a person and human beings cannot possibly fathom God's Nature. We believe, in our limited insight, that God does not exist, because we cannot see or hear, or touch the Divine.

But God is the foundation of All Being, All Existence, All Knowledge. Every atom, blade of grass, hair on your head is an extension of God Energy.

God is the Source of All Conscious Beings.

When we try to understand what God is with logical thinking we can but fail. It is like shooting an arrow at the moon, riding a bike across the ocean, or building a house with a spoon. It is not the proper tool for the task, the right vehicle for the journey.

If God exists and is Always Everywhere, then God is the only thing that can be easily known. If there is no place God is not, then no matter where you search, you will find HIM/HER/THEM.

But, we must look with what can reveal the Truth and that is not the eyes, or ears but the Conscious Mind.

Your mind is not God, but God is in your Mind,
because your Mind comes from Him.

The Kingdom of Heaven is within us and what is Heaven but where Eternal Being abides. If we would know God exists, we must seek within, for that is Where God Lives.

Where is God?
Within me.
Where am I?
Within God.

At the center of any kingdom, sits a king and without a throne, there is no realm. At the Center of the Kingdom Within Us, God Stands as our Source and without God as the Core of our Being, there is no Us.

There is no God apart from Creation.
There is no part of Creation that is not God.

But, if God is within my mind, how am I completely unaware of that Presence? The answer speaks to what God is and His Nature.

God is an invitation. He enters only where there is welcome. We were created with a free will and free mind and not even God would violate that freedom.

We are all Beings of Energy and allow in our Consciousness, only what is in alignment with our Energy field. Thoughts create our Vibrations. So, what we think and feel determines our Awareness.

Consider all the thoughts we have and beliefs we hold that stand in opposition to the idea of Eternal Being. We cannot serve two masters, we cannot be aware of one thing and its opposite together. Light and darkness are mutually exclusive, where One is the other cannot be.

But no mind is completely dark, otherwise it would cease to be. We are not a thing created that stands apart from its Creator and has its own life.

What we are is an Extension of the Thought of God. We exist in Eternal Mind and have our Life in the Universal Energy Field of God.

There is no standing apart, there is only the Oneness. But when we think thoughts that are not real and accept them as true, we separate ourselves from Reality, not in fact, but in experience. So it would seem we are something we are not.

As Eternal Beings, we chose to believe it was possible to separate from our Source, that the created could become the Creator.

In a sense it was a rebellion; a silly idea taken too seriously. Perhaps an experiment in what is possible or not. And so, the world came into existence to be that place, to experience Life apart from Eternal Oneness.

But, it was also meant to demonstrate that God goes with us wherever we go and that even here, our eternal reality is present.

The True Purpose of the world is where we can correct our misperceptions and undo false beliefs about Who and What we are and quietly return to the Greater Reality.

Remembering God

In a world of pain and suffering, war, poverty, crime, violence, and hatred, God seems quite forgotten. This is the price we pay for having a false sense of independence, for if this world is real, God is not. But God is the only Reality there is and so, the world we perceive must be an illusion.

It has been said often and now repeated again, Perception is based on belief and all belief is a choice. If we do not see the Obvious, what surrounds us, is behind us and before us, it is because we choose not to.

Honest searching always leads to understanding. But what keeps Truth from our minds is the desire to see un-Truth. We don't see God because we don't want to see Him. Rather, we pretend we are alone in all the Universe; a thing of our own making with no one to answer to but ourselves.

If we would remember HIM/HER/THEM, we must be willing to forget everything we have ever learned and accept only what is True is true.

Why do we believe God does not exist?

Is it simply we don't see Him? Or Her? Or Them? Perhaps, but we don't see gravity either and still know it is there. Rather, we fail to recognize Cause because we don't see Its Effects.

We imagine Heaven is beyond the confines of Earth, somewhere above in the clouds. Though, nothing is there but empty space. So we say it doesn't exist.

There are no saviors walking around performing miracles, just those preaching of past deeds, which may or may not be true. Much has been written in history that often exaggerates or distorts the facts. For many, belief is dependent on physical proof today. They will only believe what they can see for themselves.

Faith without personal experience is not enough to convince us. We must then find a way to prove to ourselves God is Real.

He does not take physical form and even using pronouns to describe God is an inherent distortion, a limitation of language. He is the Formless Energy that precedes all Manifestation. If we would know the Truth, we must learn how to recognize Its influence in our lives.

When we, as Spirit, decide to inhabit a physical body, we do not change our Nature. Instead, we focus our attention on the mental image of being a body. With the power given us, we gather our Energies and create the physical being we are. All of us together, make the world we see.

Matter is still Energy, in a different form and even though we may look out through physical eyes, we are never not Spirit.

If we would know with a deep certainty that God exists, then we must look for His Presence, where it can be known and understood and that is in our Minds.

If we would remember God,
we have to remember we are Spirit.

In time, to remember is to recall something that once was, but is no longer now. In timelessness, to remember is to be reminded of what still exists.

When we believe we are a body and forget we are also Energy, we have to remember. In mind, what is unremembered is not gone but is there, out of awareness. So, it must be brought back into our Consciousness.

Enlightenment, which is Awakening, is not gained by doing anything. It is about undoing what keeps us in darkness. When we remove all the obstacles preventing us from being aware of what is Always Present, we will realize what can never be truly forgotten.

Is it possible to believe we are an ego separated self and know we are part of a greater whole, that is Eternal and Unending? Of course not.

Letting go of the ego,
is the path to Remembering God.

Throughout human existence, many have taken this journey and left behind pathways, for those who came after them to follow. They are well trodden and when faithfully followed lead to Truth. It is for each person to decide how they will awaken from the mortal dream of death.

But, all have one thing in common and that is the understanding, we need to change our minds.

Meditation is a powerful way to gain mindfulness and the realization, we are not just a body, but also Energy. In experiencing ourselves as Energy, we realize our True Nature as Spirit. In that space, left empty of human preconceptions, Reality dawns on a Mind free of false beliefs. It is how the Buddha Awakened.

Prayer is a profound process of acknowledging our failures of understanding and turning within for help. It is how Jesus went from the son of man, to being the Son of God.

Forgiveness is a prayer for Enlightenment and a meditation on the Divine.

For us, Forgiveness is a way to meditate and pray and gain the insight needed to find release from all errors in thinking and the pain and suffering they bring.

In that place of peace, we can put down our swords and shields, no longer perceive an enemy waiting to kill us, join together in recognition of our Shared Being and awaken from the Dream.

The memory of God returns to the quiet mind that has given up the desire to control reality, to decide what things mean and their purpose and no longer sees themselves as fearful, guilty sinners who deserve punishment and death.

Forgiveness leads to the undoing of guilt, for it is only the belief in separation that keeps us from being unaware of Wholeness.

It is in perceiving the ego as our identity and the body as our self, that makes us think we have corrupted Truth. Yet, in doing this, we believe we have attacked God, by stealing our life from Him and fear being punished for it.

Look at the world we have made. Does it not manifest this concept in every possible detail? The guilty are punished and sentenced to some form of death, with their money or their freedom. There is no healing here or redemption in our system of justice. There is no Love or compassion and it is the ego's world because of this.

In our own life, we play out this scenario every day; on a more subtle level, but still as vicious and cruel. We judge ourselves to be unloving or hateful, a victim or victimizer, a failure, nobody and nothing and these but reflect a deeper sense of self betrayal.

When we perceive each other as a bodies with separate wills there is no Shared Being, no common Life, no One Source. Does this make you happy or afraid? Do you feel inspired and believe Life is good or life is hard? Is there any deep sense of meaning you find in the unending cycle of hunger and thirst?

No, because in this perception, there is no Unifying God that would Unite us All in Common purpose. Without the Oneness of God, life is meaningless chaos.

The Healing of Separation

If we are to find peace and happiness in life, the belief in separation must be undone. It is not conscious though, but kept hidden from our awareness, because we want to protect it and have it remain unhealed. Though, we feel its negative effects in every moment of our lives.

If we could recognize the enormous cost for maintaining the separate self, we would refuse to pay it, for It does not yield any real profit and in gaining the ego's world, we lose sight of our Soul, which is our true Treasure.

The choice for heaven or hell, guilt or innocence,

peace or war, happiness or misery,

is between the ego or God.

Is this really a choice? Who would want their own destruction? No one. But, we consistently choose the ego over God, because we are not being honest with ourselves and fail to recognize the true consequences of our decisions.

In the Light, things are seen without pretense. Fear and guilt are not Love. Attack is not power and death does not bring Life. In truth, Fear is pain and guilt is suffering. Attack only makes us powerless and death would bring the defeat of our will, not its fulfillment.

If we would find healing from all that brings us unhappiness we must take the first step and see things for what they are and decide if we want to keep them or let them go. For, He would take nothing from us we would have, but would deliver us from our illusions if we choose.

Separation is deception, held in place by what would seem to support its reality. Whenever, what we perceive outside ourselves disturbs our minds, it is a sure sign we have seen what is not there.

Fear says God cannot protect us.

Guilt says God is going to punish us.

Anger and Hatred say God does not Love us.

Death says there is no God.

Whenever we listen to our fears, believe in our guilt, indulge our anger and hatred we are testifying to the idea, we are alone, powerless and worthless, nobody and nothing because we are separate from Eternal Being.

In this mental state, God's Love would appear as an adversary, seeking to overthrow our tiny will and He would not be seen as enemy, when all He ever asks is that we call Him Friend.

If we would know God again, we need to realign our Energy with His and wipe clean our minds, from the negative thoughts that prevent the His memory from returning.

Spirit is the Thought of God.
To know our Reality is to Think Like Him.

God is forever in our Minds, but the Awareness of His Presence cannot be made known, while He is not welcome and God is only at Home, in the sacred places where Love abides.

If our minds are to be a temple, honoring the One, they need to be absent of fear and guilt, condemnation and judgment.

Forgiveness is the way
we share the Thoughts of God.

God is Love and what opposes Love opposes Him. But when our mind is dark, we do not flip a switch and turn on the Light. We cannot go from feeling fearful and guilty, to suddenly being loving and compassionate. Mind does not work this way. Energy shifts in increments.

We need to let go of negativity and find that empty space, before it can be filled with something else. All feelings are the effects of beliefs we hold and so, we must learn to neutralize those godless ideas, by reminding ourselves, we know nothing,

If we don't know what anything means, or the purpose it serves, how can we be so sure our convictions are true? This freeing of the mind, releases it from the tyranny of negative thinking and in that open space, we Invite God In, to share with us His Thoughts. We start with a simple prayer or meditation.

God, today I would not deceive myself into believing, I know what anything means. I would ask You to free me from my false conceptions and give me Your Thoughts instead. I humbly ask for the forgiveness of my errors and the Peace of Your Will. Thank you for your Love and Guidance.

Thinking with God

Do we really believe we can sin against God; corrupt His Mind with our behavior and desires and change what He created Us to be forever? For that is what we think, in the darkness of our minds and in looking out through the body's eyes, what has been done.

Whether we use these words or not, it describes the same condition. In our deepest, darkest nightmares, we fear having betrayed our Source and made ourselves to be evil, hateful sinners, whose only goal is to have a life apart from His; to destroy Him and take His place.

In fear we believe we are weak, powerless and vulnerable.

In guilt, we have corrupted God's creation.

In anger, we have the power to make someone guilty.

In hate we can separate out and destroy Oneness.

In death we triumph over God's Will.

Illusions will not go unless we look at them and it is only by seeing them with Clarity they disappear. Into obscurity we must go, with the Lamp of Truth and guided by Reason, so what is hidden there may be revealed.

God is the Light in our minds

It is only with God, can we redeem ourselves, for though we believe we have corrupted our inherent goodness, gratefully, God does not agree and would show us our eternal Innocence instead.

When we are afraid, God reminds us we are powerful.

When we feel guilty, God shows us we are already forgiven.

When we are angry, God calls to us for compassion.

When we are filled with hate, God asks that we be Healed.

When we call upon God for forgiveness, He does not see we have done something wrong and would let it go, as long as we repent of our sins. What is done in reality cannot be undone.

Rather, God would have us understand, in Truth, nothing exists that can change His Mind and so, it has no reality. True forgiveness is the recognition of the unreality of sin, of evil, of fear, guilt, anger and hatred and all that comes from them.

Salvation is simply accepting only what is True is true. What we thought we did wrong has never occurred. The Children of God, no matter their delusions and errors of false thinking, are forever Innocent. Only God can decide for Himself what things mean and it is His Will, His Creation remain forever wholly incorruptible and eternally blessed.

It matters not what we think about each other,
or even what we think about ourselves.
It only matters what God thinks,
for only that is True and everything else is illusion.

The separate self though, opposes this realization, as it clearly demonstrates, having not changed our nature, the ego does not really exist. It is an idea of separation that is not true and can easily be undone.

The ego will always point to our fear and guilt and say, "See, you are a sinner, why else would you feel this way? We have corrupted God's Mind and made our Self unworthy of His Love, by making separation reality. But, if guilt were true and separation real, they could never be undone or forgiven

Forgiveness demonstrates the unreality of separation.

We know God exists and are One with him, by seeing the effects His Presence brings. In our Minds, when we turn within and ask for release from the suffering our thoughts bring, we are answered by another idea that brings peace instead.

It cannot be that we caused ourselves pain and also healed it. It is not possible we create a problem and then find the solution alone. There must be something else within us that reaches beyond our false perceptions to Greater Understanding; that our Minds can be healed shows we are not alone.

Jesus demonstrated he was One with God, by the miracles he performed. It was not his power, but the Power of God through him that healed many.

Buddha also performed many miracles throughout his lifetime, as an effect of his Divine Enlightenment.

If we too are One with God, is it not reasonable to think we can also perform miracles? Yes and we can, though perhaps not at the same level as a truly Awakened One.

The miracles we perform, with God, are found in the forgiveness we offer the world. When we seek to heal inner pain and have our thoughts corrected, that transformation is rightly called miraculous. It transcends our false and thinking and restores us to Life.

Miracles are those changes in thought that undo our beliefs in sickness and even death itself is overcome.

To forgive is a miracle, done with God's Power.
You know God is With you, by the miracles that are done,
through your forgiveness.

God's Will

Would you know what God thinks about you? You have but ask and He will tell you What You Are. Would you know what your purpose is? But turn to Him and He will reveal His Will for you.

In the realization of God's Will, is the knowledge of our Creation. Free will does not mean we can decide what we are. It only means we can accept Truth or deny it.

When we think our will cannot be fulfilled and feel all the negative emotions that result, it is because we also believe our will and God's Will are not the same.

Who could possibly imagine that anything is impossible to God? When we imagine things are not possible for us, it is that we and God are not One.

The separate self would seem to have its own life, for it is thinking we want to be separate, that means we have a will unlike God's.

What the ego wants and what God Wills are not the same.

The ego wants us to be guilty of the sin of attacking God and defeating His Will, for in that is the ego given reality.

The ego wants us to tremble in fear, looking over our shoulder, awaiting to be punished for our sins.

The ego wants our false perceptions to be unforgivable, rather than mistakes that can be corrected.

The ego wants us to be sick, so the feeble body imprisons our minds and demonstrates Eternal Energy can not be our Nature.

The ego wants the future to be like the past, with no real present at all, to maintain the continuity of its existence.

The ego want us to be lacking, for Abundance comes from God and if we are poor, how can we be entitled to what belongs to Him?

The ego want us to have nothing and be nothing - to be powerless and worthless.

The ego wants us to be a victim and that Life is hard and a constant struggle.

If we look at our life in honesty, can we not see the reflections of these motivations playing out in one form or another. It does not matter what our social standing is, how much money we have, where we live or the color of our skin. We all have the same human life. No one is special. No one is different. We all are born in pain, live in pain and die in pain.

All this and more does the ego seek, in its vain attempts to gain reality and prove to us separation is real.

But, this need not be its extent and while this is our experience, it is not all of our Experience. We can, if we choose open another door and travel a different road, that leads away from conflict and towards peace, transcends mortality and touches the edges of Eternity, for none of that is God's Will.

It is God's Will, to have us know we cannot sin and nothing can change His Creation. As it was created, so it remains.

Fear and guilt are not real, but are illusions in our mind, not in His. There is nothing to ever fear and guilt is always insane.

Sickness and disease are not His Will for us.

God's Will places us in the Eternal Present and not the past or the future defines us now.

Abundance and well being is the Will of God for All.

It is God's Will that we share in His Power. We can never be a victim, we are the creator of our Life. When we ask, we receive. When we call, we are Answered.

It is God's Will, we are forever part of His Life and share in His Being. We are eternally One.

When we choose not to accept the ego's wishes as what we want and seek forgiveness instead, to follow God's Will, we come into a profound understanding.

God's Will and my will are One.
If they are the same,
then separation cannot be true
and is not real.

Is not everything we do not want in our Life, apparent in what the ego seeks?

Is not everything we desire, hope for, dream about and wish we had with our whole being, found in what God wills for us?

God's Will rules the Universe.
Only by following Him are we fulfilled.
Only by listening to His Voice are we at peace.
Only God can lead us to happiness.

The Return to Self

The ego has no real power to do anything. It is not a thing in itself. It is part of our belief about what we are. Whatever it seems to do, comes from the power of our Minds, given us in our Creation. It has no being of its own.

It is a miscreation, an insane idea that cannot change reality, but only keeps us distracted from our actual Existence, while we want to believe in it.

We think being a separated self can get us something we want, to somehow make us more than we are and have a greater life than we can have in God. That is why we are born into the world, to answer the one question we need to ask, "Has it ever brought us anything of real value?"

**If we would Know who we are,
we must forsake what we are not.**

The ego can never be reconciled with the Self God Created for us as Us. It cannot be saved. It cannot be redeemed. It can only be quietly and gently let go, in the calm recognition that it never was, nor could ever be our Truth.

When it came time for Jesus to begin his ministry, he was baptized by John and then led into the desert by the Holy Spirit, where he fasted for many days and nights.

Nearing the end of his ordeal, hungry and thirsty, the devil (the ego) appeared to him and said, "If you are really the son of God, then turn these stones into bread."

But Jesus answered, "Man shall not live by bread alone, but by the word of God." For he knew the body was not the seat of His Self and his Life came not from the world, but from God. To satisfy it alone, would still leave him starving.

Then the devil took him to the holy city and had him stand at the tallest part of the temple and said, "If you are really the Son of God, throw yourself down, for it is written that God will send His angels to save you."

But again, Jesus answered, "It is also written, that you shall not put the Lord your God to the test." In the understanding, what we give power to has reality for us; not to be faithless to God, but have faith in His Will.

Finally, the devil brought Jesus to a very high mountain and showed him the kingdoms of the Earth and their splendor. "All this I will give to you," he said. If you bow down and worship me."

Jesus looked out upon the world and saw that it was an illusion of riches. All that was there, was of no true worth, for everything in time eventually turns to dust. He would be king of nothing and instead, he chose to be in His Father's Kingdom, where there is real value, because it alone is true.

"Worship the Lord your God, and serve him only." He said and the devil disappeared. Then, angels came and ministered unto him, as he completely embraced his Eternal Self, that God was His Father and he was Christ, His Son.

After many years of spiritual practice, Siddhartha Gautama, came to rest under a Bodhi Tree, vowing either to achieve full Enlightenment or die.

As he mediated on all that he learned, Mara, the Lord of Illusion came to tempt him away from his task. For, if Siddhartha Awakened, he would realize the illusory nature of the world and the ego.

Mara (the ego) first tempted him with four beautiful maidens, jeweled and perfumed, sultry dancing, calling to join them in physical pleasure. But he was unmoved, recognizing the transitory nature of such pleasure and its inherent dissatisfaction.

Mara, enraged by his refusal, brought forth his armies and tried to attack Siddhartha with arrows and fire. But again he remained unmoved, without defending himself as a body, he gave no reality to fear and was at peace.

Finally, Mara, having failed to distract Siddhartha from his goal, challenged his right to enlightenment. "Who are you to be in my seat?" He questioned and all the armies behind shouted in support that enlightenment belonged to Mara alone. "Who will speak for you?" they asked.

Siddhartha calmly, extended his right hand and touched the Earth. The ground trembled and the Earth Itself spoke, "I bear witness!" In that moment, Mara the ego, disappeared and the Buddha awakened to the reality of his True Eternal Nature and remembered God.

Our Purpose

For us, God is remembered in quiet ways. We, who walk the Earth and live an ordinary life, do not have profound Visions as some prophets do. Most are not capable of that and neither is it necessary.

How can we go from spending a whole lifetime believing in mortality, to suddenly realizing our Eternal Nature and being able to still live in the world? Our task is smaller, yet still profound.

We are here to awaken the world, one life at a time and that life is ours. We do not have to be Jesus or Buddha to help make it a happier place. Our role in the Salvation from pain and suffering, is to find peace in day to day existence.

It is the individual, who seeks for their own self understanding that gives rise to change and through saving themselves, saves the world.

If we would be a Savior we must be saved.

To be Healer we must be Healed.

To Forgive, we must be forgiven.

To be a Teacher we must first be a student.

If we would have Clarity, we must give up knowing.

To realize Truth, stop seeking, for those who seek do not have and those who have do not seek. Can we find what is not lost? It is looking for it, that makes it obscure.

To regain what is already ours, we give up believing it is not in our possession. We don't search in the cupboards, under the bed, in the sofa, or out in the yard. We look in our hand. We are holding it and know it not.

Enlightenment is not a choice we make once and are done. It is a decision made over and over again. While we believe we are in the world, we will always have to decide, if we will live in falsity or Truth.

We are all under the delusion, our ego has the ability to usurp the power of God, to take for ourselves what is His alone and it is this belief which is the real source of all our fear and guilt.

In each moment we are not supremely happy, it is a moment of darkness and deception. It is then we must look within and ask, not ours, but His Will be done. For, it is only following the ego's wishes we ever suffer and in listening to its guidance, we stumble and fall.

The world is a powerful illusion, being made with Spiritual Energy and is not easily overcome, nor seen through or transcended. Because of this, Faith in God comes and goes, all at the ego's whim and when we think we are certain, we look outside ourselves and lose hope again.

But, this is the time when we can step back and see the desperate grasping of the separated self, clinging to the last vestiges of our belief in it. We know then, we have released ourselves from much and are on the steady path to Freedom.

The true purpose of human existence is to demonstrate to ourselves that we are not an ego, for it is only we who imagine we are. God's Knows we are not.

The key to salvation is in desire - what is your Will? Do you really prefer to continue believing you are a separate ego self, imprisoned in a body and destined to die? Or do you want to recognize your True Self as Unlimited Energy at One with God and All That Is?

The one goal all humans share, mostly unrecognized, but their sole reason for being here, is to awaken from the dream of mortal existence, to be still and remember.

God would teach you a lesson
and the lesson He would have you learn,
is you are forever Loved and eternally Blessed.

GOD IS

God is such a small word, it cannot begin to express the magnitude and unfathomable Nature of All That Is. It is hardly worth the effort of trying, for when we think we understand, that is when we lose understanding. But, we can and must experience what God Is in the world, if we are to appreciate Eternal Being.

Whenever you are at peace,
you have remembered that God is.

In your happiness, laughter, Joy,
you touch the reality of God.

In Love, compassion, kindness and forgiveness,
you are what God is.

In your desire to save yourself and
the world from pain and suffering,
you share the Will of God.

When you look outside yourself and see not separate bodies in opposition to each other, enemies and strangers fighting against you, a starving world of lack and poverty, limited, frail and weak. But instead, see brothers and sisters of One Family, a place of abundance, sharing a common Life, all having the same meaning and purpose, you begin to see through God's eyes.

GOD IS

GOD IS

the Father of Creation
the Mother of All that lives
the Brother of your Soul
the Sister of your Mind
your Eternal Friend

the gentle breeze, that brushes your lips,
runs through your hair.

the outward Breath of Source softly flowing across the world, on
a bright spring morning.

the warm sun melting the snow, caressing your face. the Smile
of Eternal Being, shining on that Which is Cherished.

the summer rain that falls on a parched Earth, restoring it to Life.

a soft blanket wrapped round us on a chilly morning.
the warm sweater we wear on a winter's day.
the cozy slippers on our feet after a hard week.

everything that makes you happy,
all that gives you peace
every dream you have
and hope fulfilled.

GOD IS

GOD IS

the Soul of the Universe

the Cornerstone of Existence.
the Foundation of Inner Being.
the Eternal Light within.
Our Greatest Self.

the Beacon of our Spirit
our Lamp in the darkness,
the Light at the end of the tunnel.

GOD IS

the unfathomable Joy of Being,
the deep well from
which we draw our Life.

The quiet whisper of comfort when we are sick, the small voice reminding us, it will be alright, the gentle laughter of a cherished friend, the reassurance we are not alone, we are not forsaken, we are known and understood. We are eternally Loved.

GOD IS LOVE

and everything that comes from Love

IS GOD

The Love of God

Do you believe God Loves you and feel that Love every day? Some do, most do not. In sad consequence, we deny ourselves our daily bread, for it is the Love of God that feeds our Soul and nourishes our Being.

Whenever we are afraid or feel guilty, we believe we are unloved by God.

In our anger and hatred, we have declared God does not Love us.

When we feel sick, poor, lacking, depressed, deprived in any way of anything, we blame conditions on not being blessed by the Love of God.

Is this not true? When we see someone who is successful and seems to get whatever they want and they tell us how fortunate they are, we look at our own life and our struggles and wonder, what have we done to be so cursed? Why does God not Love me as much?

It does not matter if we consciously recognize this or not, our Spirit knows. Call it by another name, it is still the same. Life is unfair. I never get break. It is so hard to get ahead. It wasn't meant to be.

God is the giver of All Things and when we feel He is not giving us what we need, does not support our will, our prayers are not answered, we believe our wills must be different.

We have learned though, belief is a choice. So, we choose to believe this, but why?

What is not loved is hated and what is hated, opposes our will. We fear God does not Love us, because we imagine, in some way, we have gone against Him and He hates us for it.

Does God love a transgressor, or sends them to hell to burn in the fires of eternal damnation?

Sin is the belief we can attack God and corrupt His Laws. But, isn't such an premise, in itself, arrogant? Who could possibly imagine, they have the Power to overthrow the Will of God?

But, there is part of us that upholds the idea as sacrosanct and that is the ego, for its whole existence depends on it.

If sin is real, the ego has reality, for what is the separated self, if not an assault on God's Oneness and the destruction of His Wholeness.

In the physical, there is much we do that is not loving and would seem evil, or unkind. So we think we can be sinners, fated to failure and misery.

The world though is a dream, an illusion of what is not possible, but we would have be. It is a child's game - a pretend life acted out on a stage, where the actors come to battle and die.

But, in our forgiveness of ourselves and each other, we clearly see what we thought occurred never did. To forgive our sins, simply means to recognize their unreality. Whatever evil we think we do, is no more than errors in perception.

The ego though, resists this realization with all the power we give it. Mistakes can be corrected, reality cannot. If the ego exists in Truth, it cannot be undone. But, if it is not true, it can be forgiven and understood to be false.

See why we, who uphold the ego, are terrified of the Love of God? If God Loves us Now, how can we be separate from Him? His Love does not support our illusions, but upholds our Truth.

To keep separation going, we have to listen to the lies of ego and hear how unworthy and powerless we are, deserving of punishment and death.

But, what a desperate and miserable Life is lived, when we feel unloved by God. This is the real hell sinners are cast into, to be tormented by their own insane thoughts.

The Love of God is found
In the letting go of the idea of sin, evil
and the separated self.

If we would feel the Love of God and remember Him, we must seek out all that tells us we are not His Beloved, look deep into the darkness of our minds and see what is truly there. For, underneath our self-condemnation, God stands, waiting patiently for our return, offering us the keys to the Kingdom of Heaven and Peace.

The Love of God is God's Love for us and ours for Him.
It is our salvation, our healing, our Life.

The Love of God, for a little while, must be expressed from one person to another. It is through us, His Love is made manifest in the world.

To feel Love, we must extend it outward. To receive It, we must give it and we give it through our forgiveness.

When we look with condemnation, in fear and anger, when we lack faith in the rightness of someone's being and mind, we lose sight of our Oneness and fail to recognize God and His Wholeness.

In our temptation to judge each other as guilty and deserving of punishment, as less worthy of love, we must step back and accept:

Our judgments are meaningless,
for God alone knows the Truth.

Then, in that gentle place, left clean of malice and hate, we no longer see enemies but brothers and sisters, companions and friends. It is there, in recognition of each other as the Children of God, we remember Him and are filled with the Light of Joy.

Finally, we come to understand, the thing we were missing and searching for our entire life, in every relationship, all our desires and hopes, was always with us, but unrecognized.

The Love of God
Is all we ever want or need.

God is
the One Truth

We are what God is
and only what God is are We.
There is nothing else to be.

In this understanding the journey ends.

In the beginning there was God
and only God.

Along the way, there was God
and only God.

At its ending, there is still God
and only God.

Welcome Home.

So it ends

There really is no ending to anything. There is only the eternal expansion of Life. Forms change and this we see with sadness and regret. But beyond appearance lies a deeper Reality. Looking through the body's eyes, we perceive a limited view. Seeing with the Soul, we have greater vision.

Our adventure together continues, as Humanity is reaching an evolution forward. Though, it is not a reckoning for past deeds as many doomsayers predict, nor is it a balancing of scales for sins long ago committed. It is a time of healing and forgiveness, a moment of compassion and understanding – it is a realization of our true Nature.

There is no condemnation here; no judgment to be laid down. There is only the soft and gentle waking up from a sleep too long slept. Eyes open, quietly greeting the sun of a new day dawning. Peace beckons and we rise up. Love calls and we rush to answer. Out we go, into the bright morning, running, laughing, arms raised up in gratitude, joyful voices singing praise to Life.

There we stand as a united Whole, in gentle rhythm breathing in and out, sharing one Source. All those hated and despised, we now see as part of our Self. Evil deeds are put aside, in recognition, only ignorance creates enemies. Those considered different are understood to be the same. The world awakens to the Truth.

My friend, let us not despair over conditions as they seem to be. There is great promise for us here. Each day there is one thing that changes for the better. Every moment, somewhere, kindness is embraced and Love smiles, as another person is freed from some long-endured suffering. They find peace and that peace spreads its wings over their life and they soar and all humanity soars with them.

Should we count up all the things that are wrong with our world and pile them up, one upon another, so high they'd blot out the Sun and cover the Earth in darkness? Or, should we count our blessings and one by one lay them down, side by side, so they build a path then a road and lastly a bridge, all can walk upon on the journey home?

I am not naïve or unrealistic. I have been a pessimist, a naysayer, a realist and the most practical person. I have hated the world, hated my neighbors and hated myself for what I thought was wrong and unfair. It has taken me a lifetime to be convinced, what is written here is true and if I, who at least was willing to listen, still took so long, what then of those who are closed to change? They would rather die defending their position.

Things won't progress overnight. Too many people have put energy into believing in separation and division. Too many nations, in their false self-interest, make their wars on the world. Peace cannot come to us, while we believe what we do to others, touches us not. There is still much work ahead. But beliefs can change, this I know and here lies our greatest hope.

Everything that is done, affects us all in some way, because we share One Life. When will the world realize this? Only when it is ready. When will it be ready? That day will come, not in a shout, but a whisper. It will pass by unnoticed, because its happening will be the next inevitable step we take. Before the sun rises, light fills the sky. The night is gone, as the morning begins; one moment becomes brighter than the last, until finally the dawn breaks.

To be happy, we need not wait on others to wake up. Let them sleep while they choose sleep. But in their dreams and through the open window of their mind, they will hear the laughter of our joyful gathering. Something within them will stir and they too, will put aside illusions and rise from their beds, to join us in living the real Life we are all meant to live, to be the awakened Beings we are destined to be, for there is a Greatness is everyone.

Do nothing but this and you will change the world in ways you cannot imagine and help bring that time of Awakening one step closer:

Strive to be happy in your own life, with your own self. Look for peace, in the midst of conflict. Give love where love seems not to be. Forgive yourself for all you think are failures and forgive others for what they cannot give, cannot do. Recognize the gifts you have been given, there are many. Know you are eternally worthy of all the goodness life can offer. Reach out your hands, they will be filled.

What more can be asked of you or anyone? It is already done the instant we wish it were different, because everything is created together. Now, we must live it day by day. Each time we choose love over fear, peace over war, acceptance over condemnation, a little more light gathers around us, until we ourselves, become the shining beacons of hope for a new age.

Go now, your Compassion is needed. Please go now, the world is waiting your Truth. And with our torches held high, we shall venture out into the darkness shouting, The Light has come! The Light has come! The Light has finally come and all Humanity will stop and bear witness to you.

With my deepest gratitude
for listening,
your eternal friend

Steven

About Me

It is traditional for an Author to have a biography at the end of their book. Though, the material facts of my life seem less relevant than the Words I speak, as they are just momentary notes in my eternal story. In the end, only Truth matters.

But, I would share with you all my humanness, because it gives context to the work. I will not pretend to be something I am not, just to appear more than I am. If this work is to be useful, then above all else, it must be honest.

I grew up in a lower middle class family in a suburb of New York City. Both my parents worked, or should I say my mother worked and my father struggled to keep a job. He was an alcoholic my entire childhood.

My cousin used to say, "Insanity doesn't run in our family, it gallops." But what can you expect from a large group of poor Irish kids raised in the depression?

I went to catholic school, was an altar boy and a boy scout. I grew up in the 60s in a different society. My brother and I walked the long distance to school every day, by ourselves. There was no fear of being abducted. We had more freedom and the world seemed safer then.

Saturday mornings began watching cartoons, with the rest of the day spent playing sports or riding bikes miles away on some adventure. All our parents ever said was, "be home by dark." We lived our lives outside on the paved streets and playgrounds. I saw kindness and caring, but also violence and chaos.

Looking back, I had a great childhood, aside from my family life. It was only at home I despaired.

Many people say their parents did the best they could. But no, sometimes they don't. My mother tried with birthdays and Christmas. It was never enough though, to make me feel loved and secure. For me, they failed miserably and never took responsibility for the pain they caused. So, while they lived, I could never completely forgive them.

As teenagers we discovered drinking and drugs. Though, I began having experiences I didn't understand and wasn't ready for at the time. So, I had to give it all up, because I was literally scared straight. But my group of friends continued. Eventually, hanging out with them became intolerable and I withdrew into myself, spending more of my time alone.

For some reason, I always had an interest in otherworldly things. I was fascinated with psychics and the afterlife. Gradually, I discovered other aspects of spirituality. In High School my peers were reading comic books and I was immersed in the Seth Material and Eastern Mysticism. It was then I started to write and suddenly felt awake - aware of life in a different way.

I would sneak into the city to take dream workshops and attend spiritual meetings. What friends I had just didn't get me and for a long time I felt like an outsider. At that age, being different was no blessing.

I was driven though, to find a deeper understanding of Life. I bore the heavy burden of having grown up with an abusive father and absentee mother. I had an overwhelming sense of guilt and unworthiness I could not bear. For many long years I felt like a wounded soul and believed there was something fundamentally wrong with me that could never be fixed.

But, far in the distance, I could see a small glimmer of light, dim perhaps, though still shining in the darkness and I knew if I reached It, I would find the Answers I so desperately needed.

So began a journey that has lasted me a lifetime. Along the way, slowly, Something saved me, Something healed me and gently brought me back to the inherent goodness of myself. Little by little one thought at a time, I discovered there was more to me than what circumstances would show, or others declared.

It has taken me many decades to return to the sanity of my Right Mind. But I am here now and have long since stepped out from the shadows of fear and guilt to stand fully in the Light of Love and Peace. I know, beyond doubt, if there was hope for me, there is hope for anyone.

A great lesson I was taught is that the past can never be made right. But we can learn to transcend it and let it go. Forgiveness, in the traditional sense becomes unnecessary, because we see no matter what we endure it changes not the purity of our Inner Beingness.

Suffering does not lead to Truth. But the desire to be free of it does, for it is only through our Will we come to know ourself. And what is our Will but to be happy in the deep surety of our existence. This is true Healing.

I was born on this Earth with challenges to meet and it was only from certain experiences, would I be compelled to overcome them. A comfortable lifestyle does not foster an intense desire for seeking answers. It may offer growth, but not the deeper yearning that leads to Truth.

Such a path as mine, requires great fortitude and compassion. Though sometimes passes through beautiful meadows, it is mostly walked in shadowed valleys, stumbling through dark caves and climbing mountains, oftentimes backwards.

There is no ideal life lived here and whether we are in the right or wrong, we all have both enemies and friends; by some considered to be the worst imaginable and others the best intended. This is the very essence of the ego-God duality that characterizes human existence. It is unavoidable.

In all my years, the one person I had to forgive most often, time and again, has been me, not just for my mistakes, but for believing in illusions about who I am. I have learned, by forgiving ourself, we can find freedom from the tyranny of self-defeating thoughts.

But it was meant to be this way, for without that deeper pain, I would not have persisted. Without a vision of a distant Hope, I could not persevere and reach the peaks. At the summit, looking down across the landscape below, I can see the whole world and in gazing up, the vast Universe and it is there I find the meaning of my life and of Life Itself.

And isn't this the understanding most seek? I did it for me, but also for you.

To be a Savior, a Healer, a Helper, you have to thoroughly understand what needs to be saved, to be healed and to be helped. When you see the Light within, this is what you are, because you recognize the Light is in Everyone, though obscure. It then becomes your purpose to ignite the fires of recognition in others, who are part of your Self.

Who am I? In Truth, I am an Eternal Being who is here to make manifest my Enlightenment, for it is only by giving that we receive.

I live an ordinary life, but with moments of extraordinary insight. I am profoundly creative and Clarity is my Art. I have done the work necessary to achieve greater Understanding and in my certainty, I cannot be moved. This is the part I play, in the great Crusade to undo Illusions and heal the fractured picture of Humanity.

I connect with my Higher Self and remember the Grace of God, the Lord of Heaven, the Goddess of Wisdom, my beloved Friend, the Deep Well of Joy from which I draw Life.

So, I too am a Voice for Love in the World, a Speaker of Wisdom who serves the Oneness from which we come. I am Energy but not its Source. Like many others, I hold a Lamp that shines in the night, welcoming all on their journey Home.

But there is nothing special about me and that is my greatest gift to you - the realization of our sameness.

This book is yours, as much as it is mine. Without your attention, it has no meaning. You found it for a reason. The Greater Source led you here, that something within these pages may be a bridge between you and You – an open doorway through which your own deeper knowing may flow. You can understand this work, because the Light is in you, as it is in me.

I bear witness, that regardless of the circumstances we find ourselves in, we are never abandoned to the darkness and give testimony that our Eternal Reality goes with us, wherever we seem to be.

As it has been given me, I would give you all that I have learned that you might make it your own and so gain the happiness that is the rightful inheritance of all God's glorious Children.

If you would truly know who I am, then know who You are and together, we may celebrate the Greater Being we All share.

We are all Eternally Innocent
and forever Blessed.
We are the Beloved of God
This is our Truth.

Now we kneel together,
in the place we stand as One,
in unfathomable gratitude to
The Great Creator of All That Is
for Life.

This is our final prayer,
in Celebration.

Thank you for our Strength and Power.
Thank you for your Love and Glory.
Thank you for making Life so Beautiful.
Thank you for the Joy and Everything.

And now we rise and say,
Amen.

Thy Will is done.

Made in the USA
Middletown, DE
04 March 2023

26109258R00161